START YOUR OWN
MICROBREWERY, DISTILLERY, OR CIDERY

Additional titles in **Entrepreneur's Startup Series**

Start Your Own

Entrepreneur
MAGAZINE'S

STARTUP

START YOUR OWN
MICROBREWERY, DISTILLERY, OR CIDERY

CRAFT BEER · CRAFT SPIRITS · ARTISAN HARD CIDER

The Staff of Entrepreneur Media, Inc. & Corie Brown
with Zester Daily Contributors

Entrepreneur
PRESS®

Entrepreneur Press, Publisher
Cover Design: Andrew Welyczko
Production and Composition: Eliot House Productions

Library of Congress Cataloging-in-Publication Data
Brown, Corie.
    Start your own micro brewery, distillery, or cidery : craft beer, craft spirits, artisan hard cider/The Staff of Entrepreneur Media Inc. and Corie Brown.
       pages cm.—(Startup series)
       ISBN-13: 978-1-59918-565-1 (paperback)
       ISBN-10: 1-59918-565-2
       1. Brewing industry. 2. New business enterprises—Management. 3. Home-based businesses—Management. I. Brown, Corie. II. Entrepreneur Media, Inc. III. Title.
HD9397.A2B7493 2015
663'.420681—dc23   2015007085

Printed in the United States of America

20 19 18 17 16 15   10 9 8 7 6 5 4 3 2 1

Contents

Chapter 3
Launching a New Craft Brand 29

Chapter 4
Regulation and Taxation 49

Chapter 5
Craft Businesses That Work 67

Chapter 6
The Craft Customer. 89

Chapter 7
Financing Craft Beverage Companies 97

Acknowledgments

The reporting for this book was a group effort by Zester Media contributors who traveled to craft breweries, distilleries, and cideries across the country to interview the artisans, owners, and supporting players driving this dynamic business sector. In particular, I would like to thank Zester's Ruth Tobias, Sylvia Wong Lewis, Terra Brockman, Emily Grosvenor, Amy Halloran, Kathy Hunt, Caroline Beck, Brooke Jackson, Julia della Croce, Susan Lutz, and Hannah Rehak. And a special thank you to Chris Fager, Zester Media's co-founder and my steady editor on this project.

This book would not have been possible without the generosity of the many craft brewers, distillers, and cider makers who welcomed us into their facilities and spent hours with us explaining their operations: Ken Grossman, founder of Sierra Nevada Brewing Company; Nicole Austin, master blender at Kings County Distillery in Brooklyn; David Walker, cofounder of Firestone Walker Brewing Company; Jim Koch, founder of Boston Beer; Steve Hindy, cofounder Brooklyn Brewery; Justin and Sarah Walsh, cofounders of June Lake Brewing; Andrew Caspary, cofounder of Ventura Spirits Company; Jörg Rupf, founder, St. George Spirits; Mike Beck, owner, Uncle John's Fruit House Winery; Ralph Erenzo, founder of Tuthilltown Spirits; Ben Roesch, owner/brewer at Wormtown Brewery; Brock Wagner, founder of Saint Arnold Brewing Company; Ron Extract, founder of Jester King Brewery; Cris Steller, executive director of the California Artisanal Distillers Guild and founder of Dry Diggings Distillery; Chris Trudeau, cofounder of Rolling Meadows Brewery; Mike Halker, president of the Florida Brewers Guild; Kent Rabish, owner of Grand Traverse Distillery; Tony Yanow and Meg Gill, cofounders of Golden Road Brewing; Charlotte Shelton, co-owner of Albemarle CiderWorks; Alan Newman, cofounder of Alchemy & Science, a division of Boston Beer Company; Melkon Khosrovian, co-owner, Greenbar Craft Distillery; Kurt Widmer, founder of Widmer Brothers Brewery and a Craft Brew Alliance director; Mark McTavish, owner of Troy Cider; Celeste Beatty, owner, Harlem Brewing; Michael Cameron, co-owner, Green Star Brewing; Greg Koch, cofounder of Stone Brewing Company; Tom Potter, cofounder of New York Distilling Company; Evan Weinberg, owner of Cismontane Brewery; Ted Fourticq, partner in M Special Brewing Company; Kelly McDonald and Mark Vickery, co-owners of Grain Station Brew Works; Dry Dock Brewing founders Kevin DeLange and Michelle Reding; Stone Brewing Company cofounder Greg Koch; David Perkins, founder of High West Distillery; Paul Hletko, founder of Few Spirits; Keith Greggor and David King, owners of Anchor Brewers & Distillers; and Brian Shanks, founder of Bold Rock Hard Cider.

We are also grateful for the knowledge and expertise shared by the many suppliers, financiers, association leaders, journalists, regulators, and other players in the craft alcoholic beverage industry: Charlie Papazian, president of the Brewers Association; Peter Toombs, president of DME Brewing Solutions; Jake Keeler, director of marketing at craft supply company BSG, Brewing Supply Group; Benj Steinman, editor of *Beer Marketer's Insights*; the staff of Brewbound; James Rodewald, author of *American Spirit: An Exploration of the Craft Distilling Revolution;* American Craft Sprits Association; Bill Owens, founder and president, American Distilling Institute; Keith Lemcke, vice president of Chicago-based Siebel Institute of Technology and marketing manager for the World Brewing Academy; Larry Clouser, northwest sales manager for Brewcraft USA; Michael Lewis, professor emeritus, Brewing Science, University of California, Davis; Krista

Johnson, the cider and craft beer buyer for K&L Wine Merchants in San Francisco; New York State Liquor Authority chairman Dennis Rosen; Eugene Pak, an attorney with the law firm of Wendel, Rosen, Black & Dean; David Fleming, a Portland, Oregon-based brewery consultant; Marcus Reed, an attorney with Miller Nash LLP; Tom McCormick, California Craft Brewers Association; Lester Jones, chief economist for the National Beer Wholesalers Association; Christian McMahan, a principal in Smartfish; David Hayslette, a marketing strategist with MeadWestvaco; Demeter Group Investment Bank, IBISWorld; Thomas Touring, director of restaurant operations for House of Blues; Dennis Hartman, manager of the craft beer department with Wine Warehouse; Lars Burkholder, regional account executive for Latin America and Brazil, Craftport; Michael Vachon, founder of Maverick Drinks; Rick Wehner, with Brewery Finance, a division of Pinnacle Capital Partners; Community and Economic Development program at the University of North Carolina School of Government; David Dupee, founder of CraftFund; Travis Benoit, founder of CrowdBrewed; Terry Cekola, founder of Colorado distributor Elite Brands; Ann George, executive director of the nonprofit, Hop Growers of America; Arthur Shapiro, former head of marketing for Seagram; Daniel Wandel with IRI Worldwide; and Leah Hutchinson, American Craft Spirits Association.

Preface

During the 2015 Super Bowl, Anheuser-Busch took a direct shot at craft beer. The Budweiser ad dismissed craft beer as a nonbeer made with "pumpkins" and craft beer drinkers as the opposite of the older, rugged men who drink Bud. Using strong alpha-male imagery, the ad portrayed Budweiser as true beer "made the hard way." As observed by numerous national publications, the ad was viewed as a declaration of war against craft beer drinkers.

And that was odd. One week earlier, Anheuser-Busch purchased its fourth craft brewery—Seattle's 50,000 barrel-a-year Elysian Brewing Company. The founders of Elysian called the anti-craft ad "tone deaf." MillerCoors, the world's second largest beer company, took the side of craft breweries, an apparent appreciation of the disastrous price they would pay if they alienated college-educated drinkers. Craft producers have been pushing up against industrial beer and spirits companies for decades in a fight to win not just store shelf space but, more importantly, the hearts and minds of American drinkers. Since 2008, craft brewers have been gaining ground against Big Beer at a spectacular pace. With the Super Bowl ad, the world's largest beer company pushed back in front of 120 million television viewers. Budweiser's new "Beer Made the Hard Way" ad campaign continued to run after the Super Bowl. The Big Beer/craft beer conflict continues to define the beer industry.

The craft alcoholic beverage industry is racing toward a future that is equal parts electrifying and terrifying. No one is certain how long today's spectacular expansion will continue or what will follow when it ends. But today's craft beer, spirits, and hard cider entrepreneurs are having the ride of a lifetime. To join them now, you will need to run fast to catch up and be prepared to hang on tight.

This book will help you decide if this wild ride is for you. And, if it is, we will show you how to survive and thrive. We reached out to dozens of craft producers—the pioneers as well as fledgling entrepreneurs, the largest craft companies and some of the smallest—to bring you their stories and, just as importantly, their advice. Each story is different and the specific advice from one insider is just that, the reflection of that person's unique point of view. As you connect these dots, you will see the larger landscape and be able to understand where you might fit into this fast-evolving industry.

There are no simple rules to follow, no foolproof formulas for success with craft. There is, however, a shared belief among craft brewers, distillers, and cider makers that even with the incredible growth in demand for craft, thirst for their products is far from sated, even in regions that seem to be bursting at the seams with craft producers. As we write this, the failure rate for craft beverage businesses is effectively zero. That will change as a rush of starry-eyed newcomers intensifies competition, making it increasingly costly to survive what will surely be a frantic next few years.

In this book, we lay out the very different challenges you will face as a newcomer to each of these three sectors. While they are seemingly similar with skilled artisans moving freely from one sector to the other—craft brewers have opened both cideries and distilleries—these sectors have their own cultures and challenges. They have separate regulatory requirements and very different cost structures. They present unique business challenges.

Beer is the most mature of these craft sectors with a unifying culture grounded in the open hostility Anheuser-Busch and other Big Beer companies have displayed toward craft. By necessity, craft brewers developed a strong mutual support system unusual in American business. They work together in small and large ways, united in their mission to grab market share from Big Beer. How Big Beer responds to its shrinking market share and falling profits will define the next phase of the craft beer revolution.

Craft distillers have no similar overarching culture. The relative newness of craft spirits is one reason. The long lead-time necessary to produce aged spirits can make distilling a far more expensive venture than brewing beer and limits the come-one-come-all camaraderie. More significantly, industrial distillers appear to have learned a lesson from the beer industry and avoid appearing to directly threaten craft distillers. Also small distillers are open to using industrially produced ingredients and often work closely with industrial spirits companies. As a result, "craft spirits" is less defined than craft beer.

Craft hard cider is the baby of the bunch, but it is a baby shot full of growth hormones. The opportunities are fantastic for new producers in this sector. But, here too, the definition of "craft" is unsettled. Ultimately, it will be a farm vs. factory fight, fresh fruit vs. fruit-flavored ingredients.

You will find investors (people who are willing to invest and offer advice) are plentiful and accessible, although relationships with them can be fraught with peril if your goal is to operate independently. The supporting players supplying equipment, ingredients, and advice are in place. Customers flock to you with little prodding. The only quick way to fail is to ignore the rules. These sectors are controlled from top to bottom by government regulation. Federal, state, county, city, even neighborhoods have a say in the production and sale of alcoholic beverages.

Today's Craft Alcoholic Beverage Industry

C raft beverages are transforming America's beer, spirits, and hard cider industries. Independent producers using high-quality ingredients to produce idiosyncratic beverages are winning the affections and pocketbooks of consumers, particularly educated, food-focused, affluent drinkers.

A handful of multinational conglomerates overwhelmingly dominate the alcoholic beverage business. Yet smaller craft producers are today's industry trendsetters. Craft beverages command a premium price over their industrially produced competition. With their emphasis on sustainable ingredients and local production, craft brands reflect the eco-values of the Millennial generation, a force driving innovation across the food and drink market.

fun fact

In the U.S., 700 craft distillery licenses have been issued with 550 distilleries in operation and 200 more in development, according to the American Distilling Institute.

For the uninitiated, the taste of emerging craft brands may be difficult to understand, changing batch to batch as craft producers experiment with recipes and processes. This has been part of craft's charm for enthusiasts who want the drink in their glass to be made with care by human hands—damn the price, inconvenience, and variability. With each new wave of innovation, ever more specialized producers are emerging to serve ever smaller niche markets.

Unlike the American wine industry's obsession with recognition for being the "best" of an established type, these craft sectors emphasize innovation and local identity. Many cities boast dozens of craft breweries, offering fans a choice of neighborhood taprooms featuring dramatically different styles and flavors of beer. Craft fans can choose a spirit made from organic, locally grown ingredients that reflects their hometown's character. A glass of craft hard cider carries the story of the handpicked apples from a nearby orchard.

► Wine Falls with Rise of Craft Beer and Spirits

New consumer research released in February 2015 shows high frequency wine drinkers shifting from wine to spirits, craft beer, and hard cider. To wit:

- ► 53 percent of high-frequency wine drinkers report choosing to drink craft beer instead of wine more often in 2014 compared to 2013.

- ► 43 percent of high-frequency wine drinkers report choosing to drink spirits instead of wine more often in 2014 compared to 2013.

Credit: Wine Market Council

In the Beginning

The modern craft movement came to life in the early 1980s when a ragtag collection of homebrewers started selling their then radically different beers. By the mid-1990s, at the crest of the first craft beer boom, craft distillers followed their lead. Craft hard cider makers jumped on the bandwagon in the last decade. By the time the economy started to crumble in 2007, a broad cross-section of Americans had upgraded their favorite libation and were crying into a better glass of liquid solace. It must have made us feel better. Starting that year, and every year since, every segment of craft alcoholic beverage has grown by double digits.

"The recession scared the hell out of everyone," says Peter Toombs, president of DME Brewing Solutions (www.dmebrewing.ca), an equipment manufacturer for small and medium-sized breweries. "Orders ceased for 90 days. Then the demand came on strong and has been steady ever since."

"More has happened in beer in the last 20 years than has ever happened to any individual market in history. We are in amazing times. We didn't see how much could change so fast," says Ken Grossman, founder of Sierra Nevada Brewing Company (www.sierranevada.com).

Spirits is a far smaller craft sector without clear sales numbers. But the number of producers is expanding rapidly, up nearly 30 percent in 2014, according to the American Distilling Institute (http://distilling.com). "New distillers can point to solid success stories," says Nicole Austin, master blender at Kings County Distillery in Brooklyn (http://kingscountydistillery.com) and a consultant to many new distilleries. "More people are willing to invest. We are a serious industry."

The craft sector of hard cider sales also are not broken out. And since cideries are licensed as wineries, it is difficult to track how many are in operation. "Cider is growing faster than any other sector," says Jake Keeler, director of marketing at BSG, Brewing Supply Group (https://bsgcraftbrewing.com), a craft supply company serving all sectors.

fun fact

At the start of 2015, there were 3,418 craft breweries in America with new breweries opening at a rate of nearly two breweries a day, according to the Brewers Association (www.brewersassociation.org). Another 2,000 craft breweries were in development. Retail sales of craft beer reached $19.6 billion in 2014 with total U.S. beer sales of $101 billion, up from $100 billion in 2013. Retail sales of beer grew 22 percent in dollar value in 2014. Craft beer accounted for 11 percent of total beer sales, by volume, and 19.4 percent, by dollar, in 2014, according to the Brewers Association.

"It has the potential to be a decent chunk of the alcoholic beverage business. There is a ton of opportunity."

Time to Jump In?

How hot is craft? Statistics from the craft beer industry, and anecdotes from other craft sectors, indicate craft alcoholic beverages is as close as it gets to a sure thing for

someone who wants to start a new business; remarkably, failure rates hover near 5 percent. By comparison, if you opened a new restaurant, you would face a 70 percent chance of the business failing in the first few years.

That no-failure rate is somewhat illusory. Craft beverage production is an exceptionally difficult business with long hours, low pay, and a painfully long lead-time before profitability. There are so few failures because the traditional craft producers are passion-driven entrepreneurs who simply refuse to fail. You need to ask yourself if you have that level of commitment. Know it will become more difficult to survive as competition increases. Since craft is hot, that competition is sure to grow. You will need (and want) to be ready to roll with the changes and pivot to position your business always on the cutting edge of craft. If that sounds like a worthwhile challenge, then buckle up!

New challenges to craft's enviable hold on American consumers will intensify the pressure on new producers. Multinational beverage conglomerates are creating more of their own "craft-ish" products that sell well to consumers who either cannot or cannot-be-bothered to tell the difference. Big companies are paying huge premiums to buy small craft producers to add craft cache to their product portfolios. Equally telling, regional craft producers are joining forces with national craft companies in an effort to stay competitive. The already difficult-to-define "craft" category is in danger of becoming a muddled. The best craft producers recognize this Achilles' heel and advocate a definition of craft that stresses transparency and full disclosure of what's in the bottle along with the provenance of its ingredients. Donning the craft mantle will require you to open your doors and be willing to demonstrate the added value of your product. Your survival will depend on a demonstrable mastery of the craft.

The good news for you is that craft is booming. Analysts anticipate another two years of rapid expansion across all craft sectors. Investors are plentiful, distributors are engaged, and the businesses supplying equipment, materials, and services are mature enough to support the craft beverage boom. Even the notoriously entrenched political forces at play in the alcoholic beverage business are shifting in favor of craft producers. Because the

▶ Top Ten Fastest Growing Craft Breweries in 2014

1. Lagunitas Brewing Company
2. Sierra Nevada Brewing Company
3. New Belgium Brewing Company
4. Stone Brewing Company
5. Ballast Point Brewing Company
6. Deschutes Brewery
7. Sweetwater Brewing Company
8. Founders Brewing Company
9. Bells Brewing Company
10. Firestone Walker Brewing Company

Source: IRI

sector creates much needed new jobs in small towns and neglected city neighborhoods across the country, craft producers are winning the fight to rewrite burdensome post-prohibition rules, even though this undercuts the power of entrenched multinational beer and liquor producers and distributors. Growth may start to slow in 2016, but it is not expected to plateau for years to come. No one is talking about a "bust" any time soon. You are picking a great time to jump into the fray. So, welcome to the party and let us help you get acquainted.

Different Products, Distinct Challenges, Dynamic Markets

The various craft sectors are not directly competitive with each other, but they do offer distinctly different lifestyles. As you think about each sector, think about your own lifestyle. What makes you happy? The craft game is a rewarding, yet long, hard slough. You want to invest your time where you are most likely to find satisfaction.

Craft is a welcoming industry thanks to a shared enthusiasm for the product and how it is made. Brewers have a communal culture and a shared sense of passion for brewing and drinking beer. You do not need a college degree to be successful and, because the industry is relatively mature, you have the option of starting out working for other brewers and finding a mentor. Almost anyone can start a small brewery and have a good chance of selling enough beer to pay the bills.

Each sector we will explore in this book, from brew to cider, offers its own unique selling points and entrepreneurial identity. Among craft distillers, you will find more stridently independent characters. It also attracts wealthier second-career folks looking to leave the rat race and produce something tangible. The long horizon requires deep pockets and rewards the patience that comes with maturity. At the same time there are hidden economies with spirits production that can lower startup expenses. Some call these shortcuts a form of cheating.

Artisan hard cider is a farmer's dream, allowing someone with access to an apple orchard to create a high-margin product they can sell out of their barn door. Those who care about where their food is grown and who grows it, find craft cider making particularly appealing. It is the ultimate farm-to-table product. Truly, there is a craft for everyone. Take a look at the differences and see what works best for your entrepreneurial spirit.

Craft Breweries

Craft brewing has come out of the basement and into the limelight to give traditional beer companies a run for their money. Who wouldn't want to be a part of such an exciting movement? As defined by their trade organization, the Brewers Association, craft breweries are independently owned (less than 25 percent of craft breweries are owned or controlled by an alcoholic beverage industry member that is not itself a craft brewer), producing no more than 6 million barrels of beer a year. Embracing European traditions, craft brewers use malted grains and fresh hops to revive old styles as well as to invent new ones. Craft beers provide a stark contrast to the weak quaffers the two multinational beer conglomerates Anheuser-Busch InBev (ABI, www.ab-inbev.com) and SABMiller (sabmiller. com) make using inexpensive corn or rice and highly processed hops. This is good news for anyone interested in going full-time craft and taking an anti-industrial stand; the options for startups are plenty, and you *can't* be a Busch and make it happen.

aha!

The concept of an American craft alcoholic beverage industry did not exist in 1978 when President Jimmy Carter signed the law repealing the prohibition against homebrewing. But when the teetotaling Georgian signed the bill into law, he brought homebrewers out of the shadows. It wasn't long before they started selling their beers and launched the craft movement.

History

A little-noticed post-Prohibition rule change legalizing homebrewing followed another act of Congress with an outsized effect on the craft movement. In 1976, Congress approved a $2-per-barrel reduction in the $9-per-barrel federal excise tax on beer, specifically for small breweries, in an attempt to help save the few remaining regional breweries.

That tax differential for small breweries took on greater meaning in 1991. During the Bush administration the federal excise tax on beer was doubled on beer to $18 per barrel. Yet he left the lower $7-per-barrel tax in place for the first 60,000 barrels brewed by small brewers. The tax break exists to this day. It is not only a tax incentive to start a small business; it is a critical federal support that helped establish the craft industry. Craft brewers are lobbying for a further cut in federal excise taxes for the smallest craft producers. During the first week of the new Congress in January 2015, the Small Brewer Reinvestment and Expanding Workforce Act was introduced in the House of Representatives with both Republican and Democratic sponsors. It followed the introduction of the Cider Industry Deserves Equal Regulation Act, another bill with bipartisan support. See Figure 1–1 on page 8.

Craft Beer Culture

Craft brewers have been united in their faith that a rising tide lifts all boats; the craft beer market will grow faster with more successful craft breweries. That attitude engenders a cooperative spirit among craft brewers that buoys the sector. Brewers consciously reach out to help their competitors make better beer, believing that across-the-board quality is vital to the success of the craft beer sector. Even with the blizzard of new brands coming to market, craft brewers maintain their one-for-all-and-all-for-one attitude.

"We're a new kind of capitalism with a different perspective on the end game," says Charlie Papazian, president of the Brewers Association. "We have found a way to be in business and enjoy it. A lot of people are flabbergasted by the camaraderie, the sharing among competitors." The craft model's focus on quality is "very, very different than the rest of society. We are open to doing things in a positive light. More passionate than opportunistic." Craft brewing rewards vision and unique approaches, says Papazian. "It doesn't reward followers, people who need a model. Consumers know who the owners are because they are leaders, front and center."

The approach fuels growth. The 18 breweries in operation in 1984 grew to 540 breweries by 1995. Brewpubs were the hot idea that gave rise to Governor of Colorado John Hickenlooper's Wynkoop chain of brewpubs and Gordon Biersch Brewing Company (http://gordonbiersch.com) owned by Dan Gordon and Dean Biersch. Breweries

SMALL BREW ACT
VS.
BEER ACT

Small BREW Act

The Small BREW Act is legislation supported by
the Brewers Association that would reduce
federal excise taxes for America's small and
independent craft brewers.

BEER Act

The Beer Institute & NBWA support the BEER Act,
alternate excise tax legislation that contains
several problematic issues which render it an
unacceptable policy proposal

◄ CREATES JOBS

110,000
American Workers
employed by
3,200
American Main Street Brewers

▲ Up 10,000+ jobs from 2008-2013

HELPS COMPANIES THAT CUT JOBS ►

ONLY 25,000
American Workers
employed by the **2** multinational
corporate brewers
Anheuser-Busch InBev has
eliminated 5,000+ jobs since 2008

▼ Down 6,000+ jobs from 2008-2013

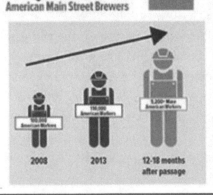

| 2008 | 2013 | 12-18 months after passage |

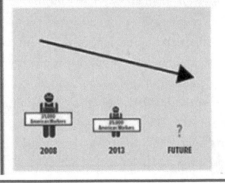

| 2008 | 2013 | FUTURE |

FIGURE 1–1: **Craft Legislation**
A comparison of the Small Brew Act promoted by the Brewers Association and the Beer Act promoted
by the industrial beer producers, or Big Beer. *Credit*: Brewers Association

experimented with styles, opening the way for New Belgium Brewing Company (www.newbelgium.com), launched in Fort Collins, Colorado, in 1991, specializing in Belgian-style beers. Sam Calagione launched Dogfish Head Craft Brewery (www.dogfish.com) in Rehoboth Beach, Delaware, with beers flavored with fruits, coffee, and a long list of even more exotic ingredients.

It was a frenzied time that suited manic personalities, such as Tony Magee, founder of Lagunitas (https://lagunitas.com), who financed an initial miniscule brewery with money from friends and family, relying on sales and bank loans to pay for the cost of near-constant incremental expansions. The struggle was to build enough brewery capacity to serve growing demand, but not expand so fast that supply outstripped demand with capital costs becoming a lethal financial burden. Many first-time entrepreneurs fell off this tightrope.

tip

International markets are clamoring for American craft beer with exports accounting for 1.2 percent of craft revenue in 2013, triple the international sales five years earlier, according to the Brewers Association. San Diego's Stone Brewing will be the first American craft brewer to open a brewery in Europe when its Berlin facility opens in 2015.

The most successful craft breweries are now national brands. Boston Beer (Sam Adams, www.bostonbeer.com), Sierra Nevada Brewing Company, New Belgium Brewing Company (Fat Tire), Lagunitas Brewing Company, Stone Brewing Company (www.stonebrewing.com), and Green Flash Brewing Company (www.greenflashbrew.com) have opened or are planning to open second breweries as distant satellites of their original locations to facilitate national distribution.

"Craft beer has won the hearts and minds of consumers," says Benj Steinman, editor of *Beer Marketer's Insights* (www.beerinsights.com). And Anheuser-Busch and MillerCoors are not staying on the sidelines. In 2014, Anheuser-Busch bought 10 Barrel Brewing Company (www.10barrel.com), a 45,000-barrel-a-year, Bend, Oregon, craft brewery for a reported $50 million and a month later snapped up Elysian Brewing Company (www.elysianbrewing.com), a 50,000-barrel Seattle brewery. These were Anheuser-Busch's third and fourth craft purchases following Goose Island Beer Company (www.gooseisland.com) in Chicago and Blue Point Brewing Company (http://bluepointbrewing.com) on Long Island. "ABI has a rather large checkbook," Steinman says. And while these particular purchases "sent a shudder" through the tight-knit craft beer world, craft brewers should get used to seeing their comrades cash out as Anheuser-Busch and others buy "craft cred."

The big beer companies don't have much choice. Americans are buying less beer overall, with total sales volume dropping 1.3 percent in 2013, and sales remained flat in 2014. In 2014, for the first time, craft beer sales by volume eclipsed U.S. sales for Budweiser. See Figure 1–2.

"It is now clear that craft is going to play a significant role in the market," says David Walker, cofounder of Firestone Walker Brewing Company (www.firestonebeer. com) based in Paso Robles, California. "Big Beer tried and failed to make it difficult for us to survive. So they only have two choices: Invent their own craft beers or buy craft breweries. Now it gets competitive. They are going to fight for market share. They can just drop the price of their beers and the majority of consumers will still want to drink their beer. They are the elephant at our tea party."

The Future

Craft beer marketing will change quickly in a more competitive market. New craft brewers need to be big

fun fact

Since 2008, when Anheuser-Busch was sold to Brazil-based In-Bev Corp. and Miller merged with Coors, the two beer giants have lost more than 20 million barrels of beer sales volume, more than 10 percent of their overall volume, says Steinman. In that time, craft's share of the market increased from 4.2 percent to be more than 9 percent of the American beer market. Big Beer's loss has been craft beer's gain.

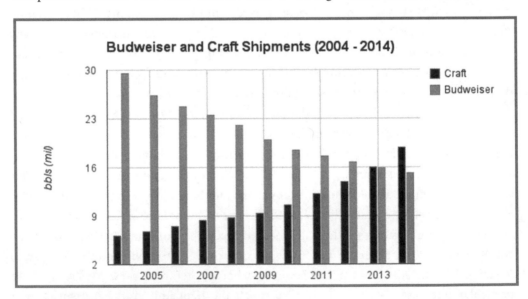

FIGURE 1–2: **Bud and Craft Shipments**
Comparison of volume sales for the craft beer sector and Anheuser-Busch's flagship Budweiser brand.
Credit: Beer Marketer's Insights

enough to finance the marketing, distribution, and sales efforts that will be increasingly critical to survival.

Craft brewers should be careful what they wish for if they want Big Beer to fade away, says Andy Thomas, CEO of Craft Brew Alliance (http://craftbrew.com), a consortium of craft beer brands—Widmer Brothers, Kona Brewing, Redhook, and Omission—in which Anheuser-Busch holds a one-third interest. Large beer companies spend an estimated $1 billion a year on mass-market, sports-oriented pro-beer messaging. Craft brands spend almost nothing on mass media. "Craft can't be cool if beer is irrelevant," Thomas told 200 craft brewers attending Brewbound (www.brewbound.com) in San Diego in December 2014. Big Beer supports the whole beer category with their mass marketing.

tip

Online craft beer trade publications to follow:

- *Craft Brewing Business* (www.craftbrewingbusiness.com)

- *Brewpublic* (www.brewpublic.com)

- *Brewbound* (www.brewbound.com)

That kind of thinking runs counter to craft beer traditionalists. In the past, new craft producers who launched with a splash before establishing a local following for their beers often failed. "Smaller startups are in it for the right reasons," says Papazian. "The larger startups, given that their investment relies on other people's money, need quick returns." They won't find them in craft beer. "No one gets rich quickly or easily in craft beer."

But they also don't fail. While the growth rate may slow, sales are predicted to continue to climb. According to industry analysts at IBISWorld (www.ibisworld.com), craft beer revenue growth will slow from the 11 percent average annual growth rate of 2008–2013 and grow an average of 5.5 percent a year between 2015 and 2020. Increasing market acceptance and low barriers to entry make this industry attractive for new businesses, the analysts say. Minimal equipment is required to brew craft beer, and it can be bought ready to use. A culture that emphasizes locally brewed craft beers has also encouraged entrants into the industry.

As a result of high demand justifying price increases, the industry is becoming more profitable. Craft brewery profits averaged 9.1 percent of revenues in 2014. During the next five years, the industry will benefit from brand recognition and increasing disposable income. There will be an estimated 4,470 breweries in operation by 2020.

Craft Distillers

As defined by their association, The American Craft Spirits Association (www.americancraftspirits.org), craft distillers are independent licensed distillers annually producing fewer than 750,000 proof gallons of spirits. They are a passionate group of independent artisans similar to those who populate the craft beer movement. In fact, many spirits producers started out as brewers, a logical progression considering the two crafts share the same initial processing steps.

History

In 1965, there was only one craft brewery, Anchor Brewing (www.anchorbrewing.com) in San Francisco, bought on impulse by 25-year-old Fritz Maytag, a descendent of the Maytag appliance family. When Maytag later launched Anchor Distilling in 1993, he became one of the first craft distillers. He learned the craft from Jörg Rupf, America's first modern craft distiller who launched St. George Spirits (www.stgeorgespirits.com) in Alameda, California, in 1982 to distill eau-de-vie from the region's bounty of fresh pears, raspberries, and cherries.

There has never been a home distilling movement similar to what drove the craft beer movement. Home stills remain illegal, a law that appears to be carved in stone as much because of the fear of exploding stills and accidental poisonings as an aversion to "demon" spirits. So the movement has grown far more slowly. There are no firm numbers on the size or value of the craft spirits sector. See Figure 1–3 on page 13.

By and large, consumers are satisfied with the products these companies produce, setting a high bar for craft producers to clear with their alternative products. It is difficult to make Kentucky bourbon as good as Maker's Mark (www.makersmark.com), produced by Beam Suntory. The popularity of the Kentucky Bourbon Trail (http://kybourbontrail.com), a state tourism board effort backed by the big distillers, attracts tourists from around the world. "People think they are visiting craft distilleries, but they aren't," says James Rodewald, author of *American Spirit: An Exploration of the Craft Distilling Revolution* (Sterling Epicure, 2014). And they don't care.

Craft Spirits Culture

Most craft distillers know this and create products that are distinctly their own: Corn whiskeys that retain a natural popcorn flavor and gins that call to mind the smells of a hike in the mountains near the distillery. A craft vodka maker might infuse his spirits with eau-de-vie made

tip

The established spirits business has consolidated in recent years and continues to grow rapidly. Diageo dominates the $70 billion U.S. spirits business. According to the Distilled Spirits Council, volume increased 2.2 percent in 2014 to 210 million cases. Pernod Ricard, Beam Suntory, Gruppo Campari, and Brown-Foreman are the other major players.

CONSUMPTION - Spirits: 000s 9 Litre Cases

000s 9 Litre Cases	2004	2009	2010	2011	2012	2013	F'Cast 2014	CAGR 04-13	CAGR 09-13	CAGR 12-13
Spirit Total	160,517.25	182,115.75	186,042.25	191,262.75	199,039.95	204,403.00	208,797.25	2.7%	2.9%	2.7%
Whisky	43,833.00	45,068.25	45,382.75	46,509.75	48,363.75	50,542.00	52,502.50	1.6%	2.9%	4.5%
- Scotch Whisky	8,645.00	8,090.00	8,005.25	8,195.00	8,265.00	8,520.00	8,580.00	-0.2%	1.3%	3.1%
- US Whiskey	19,274.25	20,429.00	20,655.00	21,513.00	22,820.00	23,932.00	25,430.00	2.4%	4.0%	4.9%
- Canadian Whisky	15,378.00	15,390.00	15,308.00	15,060.00	15,175.00	15,610.00	15,650.00	0.2%	0.4%	2.9%
- Irish Whiskey	534.50	1,155.00	1,409.00	1,735.00	2,095.00	2,470.00	2,830.00	18.5%	20.9%	17.9%
- Other Whisky	1.25	4.25	5.50	6.75	8.75	10.00	12.50	26.0%	23.9%	14.3%
Gin / Genever	11,005.00	10,982.25	10,589.50	10,417.75	10,570.00	10,343.25	10,170.00	-0.7%	-1.5%	-2.1%
- Gin	11,005.00	10,980.00	10,587.00	10,415.00	10,566.50	10,338.25	10,165.00	-0.7%	-1.5%	-2.2%
- Genever	Min	2.25	2.50	2.75	3.50	5.00	5.00	1,444.5%	22.1%	42.9%
Vodka	44,446.75	58,655.00	61,845.00	65,455.00	69,435.00	70,725.00	71,930.00	5.3%	4.8%	1.9%
- Traditional Vodka	39,516.75	50,770.00	52,530.00	53,620.00	55,470.00	56,212.00	56,760.00	4.0%	2.6%	1.3%
- Flavoured Vodka	4,930.00	7,885.00	9,315.00	11,835.00	13,965.00	14,513.00	15,170.00	12.7%	16.5%	3.9%
Tequila	8,427.50	11,204.00	11,865.00	12,419.00	13,094.00	13,910.00	14,510.00	5.7%	5.6%	6.2%
- White Tequila	1,890.00	3,585.00	4,080.00	4,730.00	5,345.00	6,000.00	6,560.00	13.7%	13.7%	12.3%
- Gold Tequila	6,508.50	7,592.00	7,750.00	7,651.00	7,704.00	7,835.00	7,855.00	2.1%	0.8%	1.7%
- Mezcal	29.00	27.00	35.00	38.00	45.00	75.00	95.00	11.1%	29.1%	66.7%
National Spirits	52.00	76.00	98.25	178.50	397.00	966.75	1,313.00	38.4%	88.9%	143.5%
- Aquavit	12.00	8.00	8.25	8.50	9.00	11.75	13.00	-0.2%	10.1%	10.6%
- Shochu / Soju	40.00	43.00	40.00	45.00	48.00	50.00	50.00	2.5%	3.8%	4.2%
- Other White Spirits	-	25.00	50.00	125.00	340.00	905.00	1,250.00	Nil	145.3%	166.2%
Rum	19,240.25	22,656.25	23,098.00	23,055.00	23,092.00	23,150.00	22,975.00	2.1%	0.5%	0.3%
- White Rum	8,199.00	8,634.00	8,665.00	8,365.00	8,100.00	8,025.00	7,875.00	-0.2%	-1.8%	-0.9%
- Dark Rum	4,321.00	4,662.25	4,633.00	4,675.00	4,584.50	4,580.00	4,535.00	0.6%	-0.4%	-0.1%
- Flavoured Rum	6,720.25	9,360.00	9,800.00	10,015.00	10,407.50	10,545.00	10,565.00	5.1%	3.0%	1.3%
Cane	206.00	175.00	145.00	125.00	125.00	129.00	135.00	-5.1%	-7.3%	3.2%
Brandy	10,175.75	10,422.75	10,363.50	10,176.75	10,327.50	10,460.00	10,571.50	0.3%	0.1%	1.3%
- Cognac / Armagnac	3,528.25	3,400.50	3,424.75	3,421.25	3,579.00	3,640.00	3,764.00	0.3%	1.7%	1.7%
- Other Brandy	6,647.50	7,022.25	6,938.75	6,755.50	6,748.50	6,820.00	6,807.50	0.3%	-0.7%	1.1%
Flavoured Spirits	23,131.00	22,876.25	22,655.25	22,926.00	23,635.70	24,177.00	24,690.25	0.5%	1.4%	2.3%
- Liqueurs	20,699.75	19,613.50	19,458.00	19,804.75	20,583.25	21,212.50	21,796.00	0.3%	2.0%	3.1%
- Bitters / Spirit Aperitifs	1,966.50	2,784.00	2,743.00	2,680.50	2,622.50	2,532.00	2,455.00	2.8%	-2.3%	-3.5%
- Aniseed	419.75	420.75	394.50	375.50	360.50	360.00	363.25	-1.7%	3.0%	0.1%
- Fruit Eaux de Vie	45.00	58.00	59.75	65.25	69.45	72.50	76.00	5.4%	5.7%	4.4%
Other Spirits	-	-	-	-	-	-	-			
Mixed Drinks	69,905.00	61,325.00	69,500.00	73,830.00	81,420.00	95,430.00	101,610.00	3.5%	11.7%	17.2%

Source: IWSR Calculations based on trade comment.

FIGURE 1–3: **Spirit Sales**

The rising sales of spirits from 2009 to 2014, according to IWSR.

with fresh local fruit. Whiskeys produced from unusual grains and aged in small casks are popular. Gins are a particularly exciting category for American craft producers because, beyond the presence of juniper in the herbal infusion, there is wide latitude on botanical ingredients. Each gin can taste unique.

Many of the best-known small spirits producers—such as Hudson Valley-based Tuthilltown Spirits (www.tuthilltown.com), Chicago-based Few Spirits (www.fewspirits.com), and New York Distilling Company (www.brooklynbooze.com)—are members of the two-year-old American Craft Sprits Association (ACSA). The association hosted its second annual trade show in February 2015 and is leading the charge to change federal and state laws hobbling the growth of craft spirits. "We are just at the beginning stages of organizing the craft spirits industry," says Leah Hutchinson, director of operations and marketing for the nonprofit association, noting that there are parallels to the early stages of the craft beer industry. See Figure 1–4 on page 14 for more information on craft distillers.

The association evolved out of the American Distilling Institute, a private company owned by Bill Owens, a former brewer and beer trade publisher who shifted gears to focus

Year	U.S. Craft Distillers
2005	52
2007	76
2011	234
2012	315
2013	425
2014	550 (est.)

FIGURE 1–4: **U.S. Craft Distillers in Production 2005–2014**
Credit: Michael Kinstlick, CEO Coppersea Distilling

on the distilling industry a dozen years ago. Owens runs the largest craft distilling trade show, which attracted 1,000 distillers, purveyors, and others interested in the sector in 2014. He publishes *American Distiller* magazine.

The Future

Owens and the nonprofit ACSA define "craft spirits" to be both grain-to-glass spirits and spirits produced using distillate made by industrial distillers. Both production processes are legal and common among large distillers. Yet, within the craft movement, using industrially produced spirits is controversial. Some "blenders," as they are sometimes called, market their products as if they produced them grain-to-glass. Two class-action lawsuits were filed in 2014 accusing leading small distillers, Tito's Handmade Vodka and Templeton Rye, of defrauding consumers with false marketing claims concerning their production processes.

"There is no self-policing yet in craft spirits," says Rodewald. No one is enforcing truth in advertising for craft spirits. "You can cheat."

The issue, however, is generally invisible to consumers. While beers are identified by their parent company—everyone knows that Anheuser-Busch makes Budweiser—consumers connect directly with specific spirits brands. Few fans of the popular Jim Beam whiskey realize the American brand is part of the Japanese spirits company,

aha!

Craft spirits trade publications to follow:

- *Artisan Spirit* magazine (www.artisanspiritmag. com)

- BevNet (www.bevnet. com)

Suntory. These kinds of deals are happening more frequently, with big spirits companies paying an estimated $1,000 per case for brands with relatively small 20,000 to 40,000 case productions.

It can be advantageous for craft producers to sell a single brand in their lineup to get the cash infusion they need to grow. Unlike the quick turnaround when brewing fresh beer, building up a craft distilling business requires large quantities of raw materials to produce a dribble of marketable product. Proper aging adds three or more years to the time it takes to get a product to market. While $250,000 and buckets of sweat equity might be enough to open a microbrewery, artisan distillers producing aged spirits often spend $5 million or more before they turn a profit.

Craft Hard Cider

Hard cider was a necessity for American colonists who could not drink the fetid city water. Johnnie Appleseed thought hard cider was important enough that he walked across the country planting apple trees to give pioneers the raw material for this lightly alcoholic beverage. But while France, Spain, and England maintained their hard cider traditions— which are, respectively, slightly sweet and effervescent, vinegary, and bone dry with just a hint of the flavor of the apples, quince or pears used to make it—it fell out of favor in the U.S. 100 years ago.

History

The convergence of the craft beer and slow food movements is bringing it back, starting in the apple-producing of New England and the Pacific Northwest, and the states of New York and Michigan. Artisan hard cider has much in common with wine, another fermented fruit drink, and the federal government as well as most states regulate it as such. Craft producers pick a variety of cider apples to give their ciders a distinct flavor profile, tannic structure, and acidity level, much as winemakers do with wine grapes. Orchards have "terroir," where the character of the land and climate are reflected in the flavor of its apples, just as wine grapes reflect particular vineyards.

The big event in hard cider has been the explosion in popularity of industrial-scale ciders. It started in the late 1990s with Vermont Hard Cider Company's Woodchuck

tip

Farm-based hard cider makers are receiving enthusiastic political support, particularly in New York, where it is a high-value product for small farmers. Fresh apples are more expensive than beer's malt and hops. But if you have an old orchard on your farm, cider can turn a marginal crop into a big moneymaker.

(http://woodchuck.com). By 2005, hard cider was gaining traction as an alternative to hefty craft beers. Anheuser-Busch, MillerCoors, and large beer importers jumped into the space, and retail sales of hard cider rose to $35 million in 2009.

Hard cider became a full-fledged phenomenon in 2011 when Boston Beer introduced Angry Orchard Hard Cider and, overnight, sales of hard cider shot to the moon, growing 92 percent by volume in 2012. Total sector sales rose to $293 million in 2013, with Angry Orchard commanding 38 percent of this zippy market, growing 80 percent in 2013, according to IBISWorld. In March 2014, Anheuser-Busch introduced Johnny Appleseed Hard Cider and MillerCoors launched Smith & Forge Hard Cider. Total hard cider sector sales grew 73 percent in 2014 to become the equivalent of 1 percent of the total beer market, by volume.

Vermont Hard Cider Company was purchased by C&C Group of Ireland for $305 million in 2012. Woodchuck sales have suffered in the now extremely competitive sector. After investing $34 million in a new Vermont production facility, Vermont Hard Cider is now 14 percent of the U.S. hard cider market by volume. See Figure 1–5 on page 17 for numbers on the hard cider business.

Artisan Hard Cider Culture

Smaller craft brands will either ride the wake of the large producers or be overwhelmed by them. So far, annual sales are up for nearly everyone. Virginia's Bold Rock Hard Cider (http://boldrock.com) sales increased 140 percent in 2014 with 200,000 cases sold. "After two years, we are among the top ten cider makers in the U.S.," says Brian Shanks, founding partner and master cider maker. Bold Rock is on track to double sales in 2015 when a second cidery is completed in Ashland, North Carolina. "We are located where we are because of the apples," he says. "Real apples mean real craft hard cider."

At their extremes, commercial and artisan hard ciders are very different products. Commercial cider uses apple juice concentrate shipped from producers as far away as China, and may include high fructose corn sweeteners and preservatives. Artisan cider uses only the juice from freshly pressed fruit. Teasing apart the two markets is difficult at this early stage of development in the hard cider sector with no separate reporting for the two sectors. The U.S. Association of Cider Makers (www.ciderassociation.org) is just beginning to organize the smaller producers. Little, if any, of the mostly farm-based artisan hard cider sales are counted in published figures.

aha!

Artisan hard cider online trade publications to follow:

- MakeCraftCider (www. makecraftcider.com)

- *Hard Cider Newsletter* (www.hardcidernews. com)

U.S. Cider Market—Domestic and Import Volumes

Year	Domestic Bulk	Domestic Package	Domestic Gallons	Import Gallons	Total Gallons	Total CE's	Domestic Growth	Import Growth	Total Growth	Import Share
2005	972	4,881,592	4,882,564	2,145,906	7,028,470	3,123,764				30.5%
2006	1,492	5,484,481	5,485,973	2,400,221	7,886,194	3,504,975	12.4%	11.9%	12.2%	30.4%
2007	558	6,128,993	6,129,551	2,711,404	8,840,955	3,929,313	11.7%	13.0%	12.1%	30.7%
2008	16,070	6,385,492	6,401,562	2,636,357	9,037,919	4,016,853	4.4%	-2.8%	2.2%	29.2%
2009	11,506	6,916,184	6,927,690	2,622,937	9,550,627	4,244,723	8.2%	-0.5%	5.7%	27.5%
2010	16,902	7,595,995	7,612,897	2,901,140	10,514,037	4,572,905	9.9%	10.6%	10.1%	27.6%
2011	117,175	9,303,780	9,420,955	3,213,360	12,634,315	5,516,157	23.7%	10.8%	20.2%	25.4%
2012	18,506	18,093,354	18,111,860	4,051,830	22,163,690	9,852,118	92.3%	26.1%	75.4%	18.3%
2013	236,188	32,080,345	32,366,952	4,908,035	37,274,987	16,569,333	78.7%	21.1%	68.2%	13.2%
2014	452,312	55,440,392	55,892,704	4,298,886	60,191,590	26,756,133	72.7%	-12.4%	61.5%	7.1%

FIGURE 1–5: **U.S. Hard Cider Market 2005 to 2013 in Gallons**

So, pick your brew. Whether you're in the mood to work with hops, fine grains, or the choicest fruit, there is a craft brewery, distillery, or cidery for you. No matter your choice, rest assured that each offers its own unique entrepreneurial landscape, cast of characters, and historical backdrop that will help contribute to your own craft story.

Making a Mark in the Craft Alcoholic Beverage Industry

C raft rewards revolutionaries, those remarkable individuals who are never satisfied with the world as it is and fearlessly seek a better way. By playing to their own strengths and believing in themselves, some of these revolutionaries become leaders.

Two of craft's earliest revolutionaries are today's undisputed leaders of the craft beverage industry—Ken

Grossman, founder of Sierra Nevada Brewing, and Jim Koch, founder of Boston Beer. They are the two remaining original craft pioneers who still own and control the companies they started. Grossman's and Koch's breweries are the top two craft producers in America. Yet it would be difficult to find two more different men. They are not close friends.

Grossman launched Sierra Nevada Pale Ale in 1981 in Chico, California, and it is today's number-two craft beer brand. Koch launched his flagship Samuel Adams beer in Boston in 1985, and it is the number-one craft brewer in America. One man shuns the spotlight while the other is the consummate salesman. One is self-educated, and the other is an Ivy Leaguer. While no one is a success on their own, both of these brewers were the singular architects of their enterprises. Take a look at their varied pedigrees and you'll find that, though different, they share a vibrant passion for the world that is craft brewing.

Get to Know Ken Grossman and Jim Koch

Ken Grossman dropped out of college to repair bicycles and then opened a shop for homebrewers in Chico, California, before building his brewery by hand from old dairy equipment he salvaged from junkyards. He put every penny he had into his brewery, which did not add up to a large investment. He and his now former partner did all the work themselves. Each of the many early expansions of Sierra Nevada—which needed to be undertaken constantly to keep up with demand for the beer—was a do-it-yourself job with Grossman holding the hammer. It was years of 12-hour days, seven days a week.

A quiet, self-effacing man, Grossman brewed Sierra Nevada Pale Ale with a skeleton staff and sold it by word of mouth. If people liked it, he figured they would tell their friends and they'd buy his beer, too. To this day, he does not buy time or space in national media. Building an environmentally sustainable brewery and providing extraordinarily generous benefits to his workers is a priority for Grossman. He is revered within the craft beer industry, although he maintains a lower profile than other brewers.

Starkly different in pedigree, Jim Koch was a Harvard MBA and Boston Consulting Group-trained entrepreneur with enough capital to believe he could conquer the beer world. Building a brick-and-mortar brewery seemed crazy to him when he could contract with existing regional breweries to make his beer. Koch saved money and still was able to brew as much beer as he could sell. That beer was consistent from the first batch, something no other early craft brewers could claim.

Koch made sales his top priority, getting Sam Adams into stores across the country. He built a sales force that remains the envy of the craft beer industry, and he supported them with national advertising in print and on television. A fierce competitor, Koch took a David vs. Goliath approach to Big Beer, happily slinging stones at the Big Beer companies from his earliest days in business. Other craft brewers considered him an equal opportunity offender. When he slapped "Best Beer in America" on his label after winning an early craft beer contest, he also made enemies within the craft ranks.

Both Grossman's and Koch's companies grew quickly in the years up to 1995 when Wall Street discovered craft beer and investment money started to flow freely. Koch took Boston Beer public that year, raising $86.1 million for a company with net income of $5.9 million on revenues of $151.3 million, producing roughly one million barrels of beer annually.

But there was a price to pay for his bravura. When Anheuser-Busch launched an aggressive national ad campaign slamming Boston Beer for brewing Sam Adams at industrial breweries in, *gasp*, Philadelphia, his fellow craft brewers distanced themselves from Koch. The whole craft sector lost steam, with sales hitting a plateau that lasted nearly a decade.

At the same time Koch launched his IPO, Grossman desperately needed $30 million to build a new brewery that could produce the 600,000 barrels a year necessary to sustain Sierra Nevada's then double-digit growth rate. For two years, he talked with investors and considered launching an IPO himself. Ultimately, he rejected the idea of answering to outside investors. In 1997, he took out an expensive bank loan, severed ties with his partner and soldiered on alone.

That bet paid off. At the end of 2014, privately held Sierra Nevada Brewing's revenues increased 25 percent to reach $250 million on 1.1 million barrels of beer, according to the company. That year, Sierra Nevada represented more than 4 percent of the overall craft beer market, according to IBISWorld analysts. Grossman opened a second brewery in North Carolina in 2014 to support national distribution of Sierra Nevada, and he revamped his main brewery in Chico, California, to increase production. The company produced beer with no sideline businesses.

Koch controlled the publicly traded Boston Beer Company and, by the end of 2014, owned many of the breweries he originally contracted to produce his beer. Boston Beer produced 2.5 million barrels of beer and commanded 18 percent of the American craft beer market in 2014, according to IBISWorld analysts. Koch created subsidiary Alchemy & Science to develop a network of microbreweries to give the company a foothold in niche markets. Boston Beer's Angry Orchard Hard Cider became the fastest-growing product in that white-hot sector with 38 percent of the market in 2013. Today, with eight different ciders, Angry Orchard is the best selling hard cider brand in the country commanding 56 percent of sales, by volume.

Are You a Koch or a Grossman?

To thrive in today's craft alcoholic beverage business, you will need to bring brains, heart, and brawn to your venture, one package with everything these two revolutionaries had individually. While your entrepreneurial personality may trend one way or the other, it's perfectly fine to identify with individual parts of each of these brewers' stories. So what if you didn't go to any Ivy League school? Who cares if you start in a basement or a converted office space? What matters is how you take those small identifiers in your own story and work them in your favor. You will need to find partners who have those qualities and skills you do not possess. You are jumping onto a very fast-moving train.

Start Prepared

There is no time to learn on the job these days. You may not need specific credentials, but you need to come to craft with enough business savvy to stay ahead of the throngs of other newcomers. Ask yourself, do you and your partners have:

- ► An understanding of the business of producing perishable goods;
- ► Detailed knowledge of alcoholic beverage production processes;
- ► The marketing savvy to stand out from a boisterous crowd of competitors;
- ► The legal skills to navigate byzantine federal, state, and local regulations;
- ► The physical strength to shoulder labor-intensive tasks;
- ► Access to a minimum of, respectively, $250,000 to open a brewery, $2.5 million to open a distillery, and an apple orchard to launch a cidery?

If the answer to any of these is "no," it may be useful to do a bit more legwork in terms of familiarizing yourself with the craft world. If the answer to all of these is "yes," then close your eyes and get ready to take the leap. You're on your way to a life in craft.

Know Yourself

Vision and stamina are the hallmarks of a successful entrepreneur. In the craft business, character counts, too. The people really do make the business, and you'll find that marketing your brand often means marketing yourself. Craft producers are self-motivated strivers who take devotion to producing high-quality specialized products to extremes. To compete, consider if you can be:

- ► Fearless when you face far better equipped and educated competitors;
- ► Steadfast in your vision despite failures and disappointments;
- ► Honest about your product and transparent in your operations;
- ► Devoted to your customers and able to honor their loyalty.

These are the hallmarks of the entrepreneurial craft spirit. Be honest with yourself about whether they are also the hallmarks of who you are as a person. Identity is everything in this business, so know yours well.

Stand Tall

Craft exists as an alternative to industrial production. Craft producers sell more than their own products; they sell the idea that craft offers a better way forward. These are insular craft communities populated with idiosyncratic folks who may have gravitated to craft because, well, they didn't really fit in elsewhere. Do you have:

▶ The generosity to embrace the craft beer tradition of supporting craft competitors;

▶ The forbearance to wait for craft distillers to establish a meaningful code of ethics;

▶ The curiosity to learn absolutely everything about your corner of the craft world;

▶ An appreciation for obsessive-compulsive colleagues who actually do know it all;

▶ The wisdom to see the coming ethnic and gender integration of craft?

Starting to see a pattern here? If so—then great. That's because there is one. Though everyone involved in the craft business brings a unique entrepreneurial story to the table, each has his or her own approach to the application of it to everyday business.

Set Goals

In addition to evaluating your strengths and weaknesses, it is important to define your business goals. For some people, the goal is the freedom to do what they want when they want, without anyone telling them otherwise. For others, the goal is financial security. When setting goals, aim for the following qualities:

▶ *Specificity.* You have a better chance of achieving a goal if it is specific. "Raising capital" isn't a specific goal; "raising $10,000 by July 1" is.

▶ *Optimism.* Be positive when you set your goals. "Being able to pay the bills" isn't exactly an inspirational goal. "Achieving financial security" phrases your goal in a more positive manner, thus firing up your energy to attain it.

▶ *Realism.* If you set a goal to earn $100,000 a month when you've never earned that much in a year, that goal is unrealistic. Begin with small steps, such as increasing your monthly income by 25 percent. Once your first goal is met, you can reach for larger ones.

▶ *Short and long term.* Short-term goals are attainable in a period of weeks to a year. Long-term goals can be for five, ten, or even 20 years; they should be substantially greater than short-term goals but should still be realistic.

The most important rule of self-evaluation and goal-setting is honesty. Going into business with your eyes wide open about your strengths and weaknesses, your likes and dislikes, and your ultimate goals lets you confront the decisions you'll face with greater confidence and a greater chance of success.

Advice from Two Leaders

Grossman and Koch live the craft creed of supporting their fellow craft producers. Both have established mentorship programs that provide training and opportunities to fledgling craft producers. They believe their own success is enhanced when other craft producers succeed. They open their breweries to tours and put freshness stamps on their products because they believe consumers should be guaranteed the best quality they can offer. They share what they have learned with the rest of the craft community because it speeds the growth and development of the sector. A rising tide lifts all boats.

Ken Grossman: Be Nimble, Be Smart

The "no failure" days are coming to an end with so many new producers jumping into the craft market. Failure can happen, and success is not a foregone conclusion in craft. According to Grossman, you will need to think fast and move quickly. Heed the words of one of the businesses' craft masters:

"Craft breweries are beginning to compete with each other on price, which has never happened before. Only the large craft brewers can afford to play that game. The national tier of craft will continue to grow, but I don't see room for dozens of brands.

"The majority of new breweries are very, very small, or they are brewpubs. At that size, they can scrape along for a long, long time. But there will be casualties, not tomorrow but two years from now. It isn't sustainable to have two new breweries open every day.

"Distribution is a challenge. There is a lot of consolidation among beer distributors, shelf space is limited, and the market is crowded. Self-distribution is a rational option for a new brewery in the right community, but it is limited.

"In the early days, we could expand pretty easily without someone on the street selling for us. That's no longer true. Distributors want you to spend money marketing and provide sales support or they won't handle your beer. You cannot start now without a decent marketing plan, unless you are a stealth brewery with cache. There are not a lot of players like the 10,000-barrel Russian River Brewing Company (http://russianriverbrewing.com) making Pliny the Elder."

Jim Koch: Make Friends

Big Beer is a fierce competitor with a lot at stake. Never forget your beer must taste great. You have to be better than Anheuser-Busch, always one step ahead of the big guys. Koch says one of the best ways to do that is to unite with other brewers.

"Life is a whole lot better if you respect and enjoy the company of your peers and colleagues. Embrace your fellow brewers with magnanimity. We will succeed together or not at all. We need to focus on growing the overall craft market.

"We should expect vigorous, effective competition from big brewers. They are good at what they do. They know how to deliver refreshment. When it comes to marketing, none of us can afford to compete with what they do. When AB went after us in 1996, we got kicked out of dozens of AB wholesalers. They launched an advertising campaign attacking me personally. I couldn't afford to take them to court. The Better Business Bureau stepped in and made them stop, but the damage was done. The whole craft category stalled. Would they do it again? I don't know. I'm sure they want a piece of what we have.

"Don't get caught up in the romantic image of craft brewing and forget about the beer. No one is buying your story. They buy your beer. Don't take your eye off of quality. Direct sales to consumers are the model for new breweries. It preserves your margins."

New Craft Brewers, Distillers, and Hard Cider Makers

To choose the right craft business for you, it helps to understand your options. Enroll in classes and learn more about each of the sectors. Discover what piques your interest.

"So many of these businesses are very, very small," says Keith Lemcke, vice president of Chicago-based Siebel Institute of Technology (www.siebelinstitute.com) and marketing manager for the World Brewing Academy (http://associate.wba-online.com). While the failure rate is effectively zero, becoming a craft producer is more costly and competitive than it was five years ago. "People come to us to start their careers. They are in their mid-20s and want to get their foot in the door by gaining some experience.

"Siebel has the highest enrollment we've had in our 140-year history. Our students are more driven, study more seriously, and their level of enthusiasm is higher with a clear focus on artistic expression and technology. Ten years ago, brewers had to hire people who offered little more than enthusiasm. Today, they can hire people with proper training."

Hard cider is such a small sector, and growing so incredibly fast, Siebel doesn't see many people willing to take the time to sit in a classroom. Distilling classes, however, are growing. It is a different crowd from the brewers, Lemcke says. "You don't find the need to share that you find in brewing."

All craft production operations create opportunities for tourism. Brewpubs, in particular, can change the nature of a neighborhood. So there is a premium on people who are outgoing enough to build connections with their communities. This comes more naturally for the brewers than the distillers, who tend to be more independent, more cerebral, says Lemcke.

"Homebrewers are 40-year-old white males," says Larry Clouser, northwest sales manager for Brewcraft USA (www.brewcraftusa.com), a major supplier of equipment and supplies to homebrewers and the full range of craft alcoholic beverage businesses. "They turn their hobby into income by starting a brewery.

"The younger generation isn't homebrewing. Their first beer was probably a craft beer, and they are going straight to starting a brewery. The ones who think there is money in beer will quickly learn the hard way that this is not a 'get rich quick' business. It takes blood, sweat, and tears to open a brewery. But there is opportunity in the South and Southwest, where craft breweries were slower to gain traction. Kansas, Missouri, Arkansas, Oklahoma; there is nothing much there yet."

Across the board, craft producers are the same people, says Jake Keeler, director of sales with BSG CraftBrewing, a leading supplier to craft breweries, distilleries and cideries. "First and foremost, they are passionate about their particular beverage. They have a personal commitment to it and the community that surrounds it. They are believers and hold true to it. It has been overwhelmingly white men, but we're seeing more ethnic diversity and more women. Craft comes out of a European tradition with a lot of manual labor, welding, cleaning, moving stuff around, electrical work. That's all the nature of the beast. There are also a lot of artists and musicians."

Interest in opening a brewery has never been higher, says Professor Emeritus Michael Lewis of the University of California, Davis, Brewing Science program. Classes in the brewery program he created are sold out through 2016. With so much competition, it will be harder to succeed, he says. "You have to have a business plan, to know why you are doing this project. The brewpub still has potential. The real opportunity is to train to be a top quality brewer, to be a valued employee at someone else's craft brewery. That's the ambition of many of our students." For more information, visit *https://extension.ucdavis. edu/areas-study/brewing*.

Step One: The Garage

If you are interested in the beer business, homebrew some beer and get a feel for the process along with some expertise. Short of taking classes at one of the many state universities now offering master brewing programs, or enrolling at the Siebel Institute in Chicago, pick up a copy of Charlie Papazian's, *The Complete Joy of Homebrewing* (Harper Collins, 2014). For more information, check out Papazian's second volume, *The Homebrewer's Companion: The Complete Joy of Homebrewing, Master's Edition* (Harper Collins, 2014).

Distilling dreamers, in a perfect world, would buy a small still and experiment in the backyard. Unfortunately, it's illegal and dangerous. But it is the time-honored way to learn the ropes. Start by picking up a copy of Colin Spoelman and David Haskell's *The Kings County Distillery Guide to Urban Moonshining: How to Make and Drink Whiskey* (New York: Abrams, 2013). The founders of Kings County Distillery tell their story and provide detailed how-to instructions. They will help you avoid blowing up the family home.

For wannabe hard cider makers, make a press and home ferment cider. Volunteer to help a cider maker who produces quality cider. Artisan hard cider is easy to make, even if it is difficult to make well. Pete Brown and Bill Bradshaw's *World's Best Ciders* (Sterling Epicure, 2013) brings the story of hard cider to life with profiles of many modern masters of the craft.

Take classes. There are new brewing, distilling, and cider-making programs opening every day in community colleges, state colleges, and universities. Here is a list of some of the more established American schools with links.

- ▶ American Distilling Institute Certification Program (http://distilling.com/resources/craft-certification/)
- ▶ Appalachian State University, North Carolina, Fermentation Sciences Program (http://fermentation.appstate.edu/)
- ▶ Better Beer Society University, Minnesota, Beer School (www.brownpapertickets.com/event/267722)
- ▶ Central Michigan University, Fermentation Science (http://media.cmich.edu/news/cmu-leads-the-way-in-michigan-and-brews-up-certificate-program-in-fermentation-science)
- ▶ Central Washington University, Craft Beer Trade Certificate (www.cwu.edu/ce/craft-beer-certificate)
- ▶ Cicerone Certification Program (http://cicerone.org)
- ▶ Colorado State University, Beverage Business Institute (http://biz.colostate.edu/bbi/Pages/default.aspx)
- ▶ Colorado State University, Zymurgy Institute (http://colostate-pueblo.edu/Communications/Media/PressReleases/2012/Pages/2-6-2012.aspx)
- ▶ Northwest Agriculture Business Center, Washington (www.agbizcenter.org/)
- ▶ Oregon State University, Professional and Continuing Education and Fermentation Science (http://oregonstate.edu/foodsci/fermentation-science-option)
- ▶ Paul Smith's College, New York, minor in craft beer studies (www.paulsmiths.edu/academics/cala)
- ▶ Portland State University, Oregon, Business of Craft Brewing (www.pdx.edu/cepe/the-business-of-craft-brewing)

▶ Regis University, Colorado, Applied Craft Brewing Certificate (www.regis.edu/RC/Academics/Degrees-and-Programs/Certificates-and-Licensures/Certificate-Craft-Brewing.aspx)

▶ San Diego State University, California, College of Extended Studies (www.ces.sdsu.edu/Pages/Engine.aspx?id=40)

▶ Siebel Institute, Illinois (www.siebelinstitute.com/)

▶ UC Davis Extension, California, Master Brewers and Professional Brewers Certificate

▶ UC San Diego Extension, California, Brewing Program (https://extension.ucdavis.edu/areas-study/brewing)

If your community college doesn't offer any craft classes, ask them to work with local producers to create one. Tell them to get with the program. It's a moneymaker.

Launching a New Craft Brand

Fledgling brands on the front lines of the craft movement have a special vantage point on what you will face in the current, real world when you try to start a craft brand. They offer invaluable insights not available anywhere else. True to the craft culture, these youthful producers are open and honest about their experiences. They have a sense of obligation to pay back the people who helped them by paying it forward to you.

Craft startups are fueled by optimism. Nothing can stop these entrepreneurs. When you hear their stories, you want to cheer them on. Craft enthusiasm is contagious. It can sustain new producers during the difficult early years. These stories detail what it takes to get a craft brand up and running.

June Lake Brewing, June Lake, California
Justin and Sarah Walsh, Owners
Opened July 2014

Snowboarding has grounded Justin Walsh since he was a kid. Many winters, he would chuck whatever he was doing and travel for three months in search of fresh tracks. The jagged Eastern Sierra peaks around June Lake, California, a sleepy resort town at the backdoor to Yosemite National Park and an hour down the road from the mighty Mammoth Mountain, became his favorite cruise.

When it was time to start a family, Walsh and his wife, Sarah, decided to leave San Diego and make June Lake their home. Avid homebrewers, they looked forward to building a tiny three-barrel brewhouse to make beer for themselves and their friends.

"The problem was work," says Walsh. "There wasn't any in June Lake." Everyone in town had six jobs, and many of their friends weren't making ends meet.

After a year of planning, the couple moved to June Lake two years ago, bringing their dream jobs with them in the form of a blueprint for a 15-barrel brewhouse that could produce 8,000 barrels of beer a year. It would be enough to serve restaurant and bar taps in neighboring Lee Vining, Mammoth Lakes, and a brewery tap room.

Living in a remote spot where the nearest Home Depot is 170 miles away and truckers won't deliver malt or hops after the first winter snowfall was not the hardest part. The difficultly was the building. The town of 600 souls

warning

In all, it took about $500,000 to launch June Lake Brewing (www.junelakebrewing. com). Along with their personal savings, years of unpaid effort, and $19,000 raised through a failed Kickstarter campaign (when they didn't meet their goal, they contacted the folks who pledged directly and raised the funds outside of Kickstarter), they also raised funds from selling a 25 percent stake in the brewery to friends and family. Beware of putting all your eggs in one fundraising basket.

had only one suitable structure: a warehouse without insulation, power, or plumbing.

An experienced contractor, Walsh organized friends to overhaul the space into a brewery with sloped cement floors for easy cleanup, a high clearance to accommodate four 30-barrel unitank fermenters, and enough structural steel to meet the seismic standards in the earthquake-prone region. Walsh, 34, worked 18-hour days for three months straight. By the time the brewery opened, he was punchy from sleep deprivation.

They opted to buy a new ready-to-run brewhouse from Premier Stainless Systems in Escondido, California, which created a production delay of eight months while the equipment was fabricated. Buying used equipment would have saved time.

Ironically, the used equipment may well have cost more. So many breweries are expanding that immediate availability trumps everything. If you find what you want on ProBrewer.com, the eBay of the craft brewing business, it can be delivered immediately. But that is a big if. This equipment sells instantly. Even banged-up stuff costs at least 25 percent more than new.

tip

Know how much you are ready to commit. What would you do if the money well ran dry, for example? Consider whether you'll be ready to push forward, even if that balance sheet is in the red. "When everything in our savings account was gone, it helped me get to that 100 percent commitment point with the brewery," says Sarah Walsh.

June Lake Brewing "is a brewery that a community built on beer," Walsh says, noting that volunteers put in thousands of hours of work in exchange for after-the-job beers and a promise that any paying jobs would be reserved for volunteers who lived in June Lake.

After six months in operation, sales were exceeding expectations and the taproom was packed every day during the summer of 2014. They parked a food truck offering Hawaiian-style soul food next to the brewery. With Mammoth Brewing Company (www.mammothbrewingco.com) already established at the neighboring ski mountain, "we've been surprised how many people found us. They sought us out," says Sarah Walsh, 30.

Beyond the taproom where they sell pints and growlers, the couple delivers kegs to June Lake and Mammoth Lakes in a Toyota pickup; at 8,000 feet, there is no need for refrigeration. "We hand deliver every account," says Justin Walsh. "If we go the extra mile with service, the bars will talk us up. The best marketing is to focus on your customers." They send occasional email newsletters, tweet regularly, and maintain a Facebook page. Their logo is strictly DIY.

Model for a New Craft Brewery

June Lake Brewing is following the model most often cited for new craft breweries at the start of 2015. They are keeping overhead low and the founders are doing much of the work themselves. It is a neighborhood-focused operation with a captive audience. This is a model that you would be wise to follow, especially if you feel your community is ripe for supporting the craft trend.

"To start a successful independent beer business today, open a community-based, nano-brewery. Supply kegs to bars, no bottling, and learn what your community wants to drink. The barriers are lower," says University of California, Davis, Professor Michael Lewis, an original guru of the craft beer industry. "Otherwise, I don't see how you can start now. Johnny-come-latelies will have to work much harder than previous generations of craft brewers."

There are 500 brewers in California, more than the next four most brewery-heavy states combined. Yet the Walsh's mountain adventure makes sense because it is grounded in their deep understanding of beer making. They were homebrewers first. Later, Sarah worked at two San Diego-area breweries and Justin had a month-long internship at Alaskan Brewing Company (http://alaskanbeer.com).

tip

Consider adding a tasting or taproom to your brew business. Brewery taprooms provide high-margin sales. Boston Beer's Jim Koch calls it "the business model of the future." Taproom beer that sells for $6 a pint translates to roughly $1,200 gross revenue a barrel of beer. After costs and fees associated with selling bottled beer through a distributor, Koch estimates the same barrel of beer might bring in as little as $200. "The only problem is you can't get bigger just selling through the taproom," Koch cautions.

Their approach is particularly low risk. They built a brewhouse with enough capacity to grow over the course of several years. And their building is spacious enough that, when they need to add brewing capacity, they can do it without a costly expansion. But they kept their monthly costs low enough that cash flow from beer sales could keep them afloat. By relying on food trucks, they avoided the cost and headache of a commercial kitchen.

Self-distributing, as the Walshs are doing, is another way to maintain higher margins. And it works well in their remote region with a limited number of on-premises clients. Most states allow small brewers to self-distribute, but distribution laws are different everywhere. And even where it is allowed, there are nuances to the regulations that can may make it difficult.

Justin and Sarah are beneficiaries of the rising-tide-lifts-all-boats craft beer culture. Visit craft breweries. Talk to brewers. Every brewhouse is different because every brewer takes a slightly different approach. Every space has different constraints. That's how everyone did it.

Advice from a Veteran
Steve Hindy, Cofounder
Brooklyn Brewery, Brooklyn, New York

"Self-distribution is the way to start a brewery and build a local craft beer brand," says Steve Hindy, cofounder of Brooklyn Brewery. He was an avid homebrewer before he and his partner Tom Potter launched Brooklyn Brewery in 1988. Hindy helped organize the Brewers Association and takes an active role in mentoring young brewers.

"For my generation, beer was a second career. This new generation is starting as soon as they are out of college. You can make a good living as a brewer. Our average salary at Brooklyn Brewery is $70,000. Twenty years ago, that kind of money was a fantasy. Back then, 300 people came to the annual craft brewers' conference. This year, there were 10,000, and every supplier in the world having anything to do with beer was there.

"New brewers begin their careers knowing they are part of a successful industry. It's a part of the larger food revolution with its focus on high-quality, artisanal, local, know-who-made-it, know-where-it-came from culture. There is a lot of support for them. If you focus locally, opportunity exists. It gets more difficult the further you get from home."

▶ Read It . . .

The Brewers Association publishes a straightforward guide to the technical aspects of brewing. Dick Cantwell's *The Brewers Association's Guide to Starting Your Own Brewery* (Brewers Publications, 2013) is an easy to follow primer.

For a livelier read, with more narrative storytelling and interviews with leading brewers from across the country: Greg Koch's *The Brewer's Apprentice: An Insider's Guide to the Art and Craft of Beer Brewing, Taught by the Masters* (Quarry Books, 2011). Koch is cofounder and CEO of Stone Brewing Company in San Diego, California. It is the best guide on the market and well worth its $25 price.

For a highly readable history of the craft beer movement: Steve Hindy's *The Craft Beer Revolution: How a Band of Microbrewers Is Transforming the World's Favorite Drink*, (St. Martin's Press, 2014) will ground a new brewer in the ever-evolving story of craft beer.

Ventura Spirits Company, Ventura, California
Andrew Caspary, Anthony Caspary, Henry Tarmy,
and James Greenspun, Owners
Opened April 2014

Andrew Caspary, 33, and his brother Anthony, 31, made a little hooch in a hobby still and considered starting a craft distillery. But they needed help. Once Andrew's Dartmouth College roommate, Henry Tarmy, 33, moved to Los Angeles with brother-in-law James Greenspun, 33, in tow, they had an MBA, an engineer, an industrial designer, and an environmentalist. Ventura Spirits was launched in 2010.

Their first sale was in mid-2014 to a cousin working in a tiny wine and cheese shop in Beverly Hills. By September, Whole Foods Market had Ventura Spirits (http://venturaspirits.com) in stores across SoCal. They were selling local, unique spirits to an eager market.

The base ingredient for their signature vodka—Ventura County strawberries—is an original move. Also unique is their copper still—a four-plate column/pot hybrid they handcrafted themselves to get the efficiency of a column still without losing the flavor preservation quality of a pot still.

Opinions differ on whether their vodka retains a hint of its strawberry origins, but it definitely has a distinct smooth, round, umami-ish mouth-feel. They could have bought neutral spirits at $6 a gallon from an industrial producer, run it once through a still, filtered out the harshness, and sold it for the same price, which is the story behind many "craft" vodkas.

"There are enough people doing that already," says Caspary. "We have a heartfelt belief that distilling is an agrarian tradition firmly rooted in place and, when every community has its own distilling tradition, the imbalances of the globalized economy will begin to correct. We want to be a part of that change."

Still, he says, there is a place for commercial base alcohol in craft spirits. Until Caspary and his team can afford a large enough distillery to produce grain spirits themselves, they are using an industrially-produced organic wheat spirit as the base for their Wilder Gin.

aha!

The strawberries are filtered to a clear juice and fermented to 10 percent alcohol. A batch of 10,000 pounds of fruit becomes 1,000 gallons of juice that is distilled six times to become 190-proof vodka. Watered-back to an 80-proof vodka, the team ends up with 850 bottles Caspary's father hand labels. It takes them two months to create a bottle that retails for $29.99.

The local/sustainable part is the purple sage, sagebrush, bay leaf, yerba santa, chuchupate, and pixie tangerine peel, some of which is foraged in the Santa Monica Mountains behind their distillery. The juniper berries and coriander seeds complete the botanicals for a 12-hour infusion, after which they let it rest for three weeks before bottling to firmly establish aromas. Then it is four weeks to market at a price of $32. The gin has smells and tastes reminiscent of a hike in the coastal hills near the ocean.

A prickly pear brandy—their version of American tequila—rounds out their portfolio for a total production of 2,700 six-bottle cases. "We're still in the beta phase," Caspary says, noting that they haven't come close to reaching their production capacity.

An aged whiskey distilled from Kernza grain, a proto-wheat developed by the ecologists at The Land Institute in Kansas as part of a project to re-establish wild prairies, is aging in oak barrels. In development is a seaweed and rice distilled spirit made with the koji yeast used in sake. They hope it will taste like the ocean out their front door.

Model for a New Craft Distillery

Distilling is less expensive—and more profitable—than brewing, if you don't count the cost of holding your inventory in oak barrels for years as you wait for it to age into sippable whiskey. It is why distillers always start by selling vodka, gin, or white (unaged) whiskey. The best marketing tool is the origin of the ingredients: local, local, local.

"Consumers are willing to pay more for spirits [than craft beer], and the upfront investment in equipment is laughably cheap, and the ingredients cost less," says Jake Keeler, director of marketing at BSG, a leading supplier of ingredients and services to craft brewers and distillers.

Caspary and his team are following the craft-distilling playbook by starting with white spirits that move quickly from still to store shelves so they can pay the bills while their brown spirits age. They are taking advantage of readily available high-quality industrial spirits to make one of the products in their portfolio, conserving time, effort, and money while still creating a unique, high-quality craft product. At the same time they are following the "craft" standard of transparency in all of their ingredients and processes.

They are riding the local, environmentally sustainable wave that is working so well in craft spirits today and doing it with products that stand out on the shelf. Retailers are lining up for their spirits, and they haven't spent a nickel on marketing. Their website is a rudimentary placeholder. They started with a home still and did not work with a commercial distiller before launching their company.

Advice from a Veteran
Jörg Rupf, Founder
St. George Spirits, Alameda, California

Jörg Rupf is America's first modern craft distiller and a specialist in eau-de-vie. He created Hangar 1 Vodka in 2002, which he infused with various fresh fruits, as well as a celebrated series of gins and whiskeys. He sold the Hangar 1 brand to Proximo Spirits, based in New Jersey in 2010.

"In some ways, I would do exactly the same thing all over again. It wasn't about business or the marketplace. I knew what I wanted to do—doing something with my hands—and it served me." In 1982, there wasn't a market for his eau-de-vie in the U.S., so he had to export most of it to Germany through a large distribution company. "This was not the cleverest or most profitable way to live, but it served me."

"Every product we make is infused with the goal to bring out the best of the main ingredient, to make it shine. We take what nature gives us and translate it in the best way possible to our spirits. We stuck with our philosophy. Lance [Winters] is carrying on this legacy. It really touches me so deeply that I can pass it on to the next generation and to someone who is like a son to me."

>
>
> **warning**
>
> Keep an eye on your money sources. "One thing I did right," says Jörg Rupf, founder, St. George Spirits, was to not take any investors. "It limited funds for growth and for living, but I didn't have to answer to anyone." If you can swing it, find funding without strings.

Brooks Dry Cider, San Francisco, California
Brooks Bennett, Owner
Opened 2014

Somewhere between the London pubs and the ones he frequented in South Africa during his college year abroad, it occurred to Brooks Bennett that English-style hard cider was a pretty great drink and there wasn't any of it back home in California. After graduating from George Washington University, Bennett began a quest to make hard cider in his home state. A summer internship at Michigan's Tandem Ciders (http://tandemciders.com) was followed by a professional cider-making course at Northwest Agriculture Business Center (www.agbizcenter.org) in Mount Vernon, Washington.

A city kid with nary an apple tree to his name, Bennett briefly considered importing hard cider from England. But it lacked the satisfaction of producing something of his own.

Living in San Francisco, he operated a pedicab to pay the rent on his Mission-district apartment while he worked on a business plan and fermented endless batches of hard cider in his kitchen. To avoid the funky flavors of some hard ciders, he uses Fuji, Honey Crip, Ginger Gold, and Granny Smith apples to make his signature light, clean-tasting libation.

A commercial orchard in Oregon sells him pressed-to-order juice. Finding a place to ferment it, however, was a saga. Bennett first connected with Crispin Cider Company (http://crispincider.com) in the Sacramento region to use their excess capacity to make his hard cider. But even as he was negotiating the deal, Crispin's hard cider sales suddenly soared. A beat later, MillerCoors bought Crispin to add hard cider to their portfolio.

tip

Some good points of reference are:

- Bill Owen's *Craft of Whiskey Distilling* (American Distilling Institute, 2013)

- James Rodewald's *American Spirit: An Exploration of the Craft Distilling Revolution* (Sterling Epicure, 2014)

Bennett could feel the rising wave of demand for hard cider as one after another cidery turned him away. He found no excess cider-making capacity at any existing cideries.

The "aha" moment was when he looked up the road to Napa, where custom crush wineries sit idle nine months of the year. In California's winemaking capital, fermenting one fruit would be just as easy as fermenting another. "It took me a year to figure that out," says Bennett. "The great thing about the winery I found is that they had experience making hard cider."

The 28-year-old entrepreneur raised $345,000 in a "friends, family, and fools" round of investment. "It comfortably launches me in the San Francisco market," he says. In fall 2014, he produced his first commercial batch: 1,400 cases (24/12-ounce bottle cases) and a couple of hundred kegs; roughly a 50/50 split to distribute between retail sales and on-premise sales at restaurants and bars. Brooks Dry Cider (http://brooksdrycider.com) was born. He can make more hard cider whenever he wants by simply custom-pressing more juice in Oregon and fermenting it in Napa where he bottles it unaged. The first batch cost $55,000 to produce. He retails a four-pack for $8.

"I want to make this work and then see about building my own cidery where I can have a taproom. That's biting off more than I can chew to start. The barriers to entry in the market are low. It's a simple process. But cider is more expensive to make than beer; the ingredients are more expensive," says Bennett.

His next step is lining up a distributor. "I'm being very careful. Going slowly. Talking to wine distributors. The hard cider segment is growing fast, so they are open to me." He is already making sales calls to bars and restaurants and expects there will be strong word-of-mouth support from friends asking for his cider in San Francisco. He also plans to sponsor events that provide an opportunity for consumers to try his hard cider. "I'm really into cycling and want to get our cider in front of people by sponsoring cool California-type stuff like cycling. One investor thinks surfing sponsorships are a perfect fit." Bennett says he understands he needs to work social media and has set up a Brooks Dry Cider Facebook page.

At this point, Bennett is still a one-man show, doing everything himself. The startup investment allows him to focus all of his energies on building the brand. He no longer peddles a pedicab to pay the rent.

Model for a New Craft Hard Cidery

You don't have to own your own farm to make craft cider. You just have to have access to the quality fruit that you'll be comfortable marketing as the primary ingredient of your cider. Take Bennett, for example. He isn't tying himself down to a farm, even though he is sticking to craft's requirement of fresh fruit (apples are typical, but pears and quince are other foundation fruits used in cider). He figured out how to have his fresh-pressed juice delivered when and where he wants it. It's still craft—it's just not farm-based craft.

"Cider is a new vertical," says Krista Johnson, the cider and craft beer buyer for K&L Wine Merchants (www.klwines.com) in San Francisco. "When something is good, the producer has to grow quickly to meet the demand. The trick is to do that without losing your soul, without compromising quality."

Great cider? To Johnson, "It's complex, dry, no residual sugar." She likes the "funky, earthy, savory tannins from the apple skins, a grown-up drink."

With so much industrial-strength activity in the hard cider sector, the difference that distinguishes a small craft producer is not yet defined. Most likely, craft will set itself apart by its fruit. Craft cider has provenance. That fruit can be bought in bulk from large

▶ Read It . . .

Beautifully illustrated and exhaustively detailed, Claude Jolicoeur's *The New Cider Maker's Handbook* (Chelsea Green Publishing, 2013) has everything necessary to start making hard cider at home. And for some history, check out the book that inspired the current hard cider revival, Ben Watson's *Cider, Hard and Sweet: History, Traditions and Making Your Own* (The Countryman Press, 2013).

orchards, pressed to order in a giant facility, shipped a thousand miles in tanker trucks to a cider house, where it is fermented into hard cider. But the process starts in an identifiable orchard. Reconstituted juice, high-fructose corn syrup, and flavor enhancers are the marks of industrial hard cider.

Advice from a Veteran
Mike Beck, *Owner*
Uncle John's Fruit House Winery, St. John's, Michigan

"I would never make a hard cider that isn't 100 percent fresh apples. It is the only way to make an artisan cider," says Mike Beck (www.ujhardcider.com), who has been making hard cider for a dozen years at his family's cidery in rural Michigan. "You can hold the apples in cold storage for months. After pressing, the juice is just beautiful. It represents the fruit of that year." Also, no self-respecting cider maker uses Red Delicious apples. "They are awful in cider. No flavor."

Just like Beck carefully chooses his apples for the most flavorful cider, so must you choose the defining elements of your craft business. No matter what kind of model you choose to follow, remember that it is ultimately your entrepreneurial spirit, identity, and worldview of the craft business that will set you apart from your competitors. The beauty (and yes, sometimes painful truth) of craft is that there is no one perfect model. It can be a crazy quilt of ideas, concepts, brews, production styles, and marketing efforts. Give yourself permission to pick and choose what advice from these veterans works best for you. One way you can solidify the concepts you choose is to create a mission statement.

Speaking of veteran advice, I'm looking to the Entrepreneur Media team for an assist with this section. They know better than anyone the best and most useful tips for crafting a strong mission statement and a winning business plan. The best part is, you can apply these tried-and-true tenets to whatever craft business model you brew up. Let's wrap up this chapter with some of their sage advice.

Go on a Mission

Now that you've gotten to know some of your predecessors, it's time to think about what kind of craft business *you* want to build. To do that, you must first think about what your "big picture" looks like. In other words, think about your mission statement.

To come up with a statement that encompasses all the major elements of your business, start with the right questions. Business plan consultants say the most important question is, "What business are you in?" Since you have already gone through the steps of creating your niche, answering this question should be easy for you.

Answering the following ten questions will help you to create a verbal picture of your craft business's mission:

1. *Why are you in the craft alcoholic beverage business?* What do you want for yourself, your family, and your customers?

   Think about the spark that ignited your decision to start a business. What will keep it burning?

2. *Who are your customers?* What can you do for them that will enrich their lives and contribute to their success—now and in the future?

3. *What image of your craft business do you want to convey?* Customers, suppliers, employees, and the public will all have perceptions of your company. How will you create the desired picture?

4. *What is the nature of your products and services?* What factors determine pricing and quality? Consider how these relate to the reasons for your business's existence. How will all this change over time?

5. *What level of service do you provide?* Most companies believe they offer "the best service available," but do your customers agree? Don't be vague; define what makes your service so extraordinary.

6. *What roles do you and your employees play?* Wise captains develop a leadership style that organizes, challenges, and recognizes employees.

7. *What kind of relationships will you maintain with suppliers and distributors?* Every business is in partnership with its suppliers. When you succeed, so do they.

8. *How do you differ from competitors?* Many entrepreneurs forget they are pursuing the same dollars as their competitors. What do you do better, cheaper, or faster than competitors? How can you use competitors' weaknesses to your advantage?

9. *How will you use technology, capital, processes, products, and services to reach your goals?* A description of your strategy will keep your energies focused on your goals.

10. *What underlying philosophies or values guided your responses to the previous questions?* Some businesses choose to list these separately. Writing them down clarifies the "why" behind your mission.

Say Something

Crafting a mission statement requires time, thought, and planning. However, the effort is well worth it. In fact, most startup entrepreneurs discover that the process of crafting the mission statement is as beneficial as the final statement itself. Going through the process will help you solidify the reasons for what you are doing and clarify the motivations behind your business.

Here are some tips to make your mission statement the best it can be:

▶ *Involve those connected to your business.* Even if you are a sole proprietor, it helps to get at least one other person's ideas for your mission statement. Other people can help you see strengths, weaknesses, and voids you might miss. If you have no partners or investors to include, consider knowledgeable family members and close friends, employees, or accountants. Choose supportive people who truly want you to succeed.

▶ *Set aside several hours*—a full day, if possible—to work on your statement. Mission statements are short—typically more than one sentence but rarely exceeding a page. Still, writing one is not a short process. It takes time to come up with language that simultaneously describes an organization's heart and soul, and serves as an inspirational beacon to everyone involved in the business.

▶ *Plan a date.* Set aside time to meet with the people who'll be helping you. Write a list of topics to discuss or think about. Find a quiet, comfortable place away from phones and interruptions.

▶ *Be prepared.* If you have several people involved, be equipped with refreshments (May we suggest a craft brew?), extra lists of topics, paper, and pencils. Explain the meaning and purpose of a mission statement before you begin—not everyone will automatically know what they're all about.

▶ *Brainstorm.* Consider every idea, no matter how silly it sounds. Stimulate ideas by looking at sample mission statements. If you're working with a group, use a flip chart to record responses so everyone can see them. Once you've finished brainstorming, ask everyone to write individual mission statements for your business. Read the statements, select the best pieces, and fit them together.

▶ *Use "radiant words."* Once you have the basic idea in writing, polish the language of your mission statement. The statement should create dynamic mental visuals and inspire action. Use offbeat, colorful verbs and adjectives to spice up your statement. Don't hesitate to drop in words like "kaleidoscope," "sizzle," "cheer," "outrageous," and "marvel" to add zest. If you want customers to "boast" about your goods and services, say so—along with the reasons why.

Once your mission statement is complete, start spreading the word. You need to convey your mission statement to others inside and outside the business to tell everyone you know where you are going and why. Print it on company materials, such as your brochures and your business plan, imprint it in your social media profiles, or even on the back of your business cards.

Creating a Winning Business Plan

The craft alcoholic beverage business is supposed to be kind of, well, anti-establishment. But if you think you don't need a full-fledged business plan to succeed, you can think again. It may be a fun business, but craft is a business all the same, and a little solid planning goes a long way. According to a recent *State of Small Business* report, commissioned by Palo Alto Software, 79 percent of companies with a business plan say they are better off financially year after year, while only a third of small businesses without a business plan can say the same thing. Additionally, nearly 75 percent of established companies that have a business plan in place expect to grow, compared to only 17 percent that don't have a business plan. That's even stronger evidence than an earlier study conducted for AT&T, showing only 42 percent of small-business owners bother to develop a formal business plan; of those who do use a plan, 69 percent say it was a major contributor to their success.

Some people think you don't need a business plan unless you're trying to borrow money. Of course, it's true that you do need a good plan if you intend to approach a lender—whether a banker, a venture capitalist, or any number of other sources—for startup capital. But a business plan is more than a pitch for financing; it's a guide to help you define and meet your business goals.

Just as you wouldn't start off on a cross-country drive without a road map, you should not embark on your new business without a business plan to guide you. A business plan won't automatically make you a success, but it will help you avoid some common causes of business failure, such as undercapitalization or lack of an adequate market.

As you research and prepare your business plan, you'll find weak spots in your business idea that you'll be able to repair. You'll also discover areas with potential you may not have thought about before—and ways to profit from them. Only by putting together a business plan can you decide whether your great idea is really worth your time and investment.

What is a business plan, and how do you put one together? Simply stated, a business plan conveys your business goals and the strategies you'll use to meet them, potential problems that may confront your business and ways to solve them, the organizational structure of your business (including titles and responsibilities), and the amount of capital required to finance your venture and keep it going until it breaks even.

Sound impressive? It can be, if put together properly. A good business plan follows generally accepted guidelines for both form and content. There are three primary parts of a business plan.

1. The first is the business concept, where you discuss the industry, your business structure, your product or service, and how you plan to make your business a success.
2. The second is the marketplace section, in which you describe and analyze potential customers: who and where they are, what makes them buy, and so on. Here, you also describe the competition and how you will position yourself to beat it.
3. Finally, the financial section contains your income and cash-flow statements, balance sheet, and other financial ratios, such as break-even analyses. This part may require help from your accountant and a good spreadsheet software program.

Breaking these three major sections down further, a business plan consists of seven major components:

1. Executive summary
2. Business description
3. Market strategies
4. Competitive analysis
5. Design and development plan
6. Operations and management plan
7. Financial factors

In addition to these sections, a business plan should also have a cover, title page, and table of contents.

Executive Summary

Anyone looking at your business plan will first want to know what kind of business you are starting. So the business concept section should start with an executive summary, which outlines and describes the product or service you will sell.

The executive summary is the first thing the reader sees. Therefore, it must make an immediate impact by clearly stating the nature of the business and, if you are seeking capital, the types of financing you want. The executive summary describes the business, its legal form of operation (sole proprietorship, partnership, corporation, or limited liability company), the amount and purpose of the loan requested, the repayment schedule, the borrower's equity share, and the debt-to-equity ratio after the loan, security, or collateral is offered. Also listed is the market value, estimated value, or price quotes for any equipment you plan to purchase with the loan proceeds.

Your executive summary should be short and businesslike—generally between half a page and one page, depending on how complicated the use of funds is.

Business Description

This section expands on the executive summary, describing your business in much greater detail. It usually starts with a description of the overall craft beer, spirits, or cider industry. How big is the industry? Why has it become so popular? What kinds of trends are responsible for the industry's growth? Prove, with statistics and anecdotal information, how much opportunity there is in the industry.

Explain the target market for your product or service, how the product will be distributed, and the business' support systems—that is, its advertising, promotions, and customer service strategies.

Next, describe your product or service. Discuss the product's applications and end users. Emphasize any unique features or variations that set your product or service apart from others in your industry.

If you're using your business plan for financing purposes, explain why the money you seek will make your business more profitable. Will you use the money to expand, to create a new product, or to buy new equipment?

Market Strategies

Here's where you define your market—its size, structure, growth prospects, trends, and sales potential. Based on research, interviews, and sales analysis, the marketplace section should focus on your customers and your competition. How much of the market will your product or service be able to capture?

The answer is tricky since so many variables influence it. Think of it as a combination of words and numbers. Write down the who, what, when, where, and why of your customers. The answer is critical to determining how you will develop pricing strategies and distribution channels.

Be sure to document how and from what sources you compiled your market information. Describe how your business fits into the overall market picture. Emphasize your unique selling proposition (USP)—in other words, what makes you different? Explain why your approach is ideal for your market

Once you've clearly defined your market and established your sales goals, present the strategies you'll use to meet those goals.

▶ *Price.* Thoroughly explain your pricing strategy and how it will affect the success of your product or service. Describe your projected costs and then determine pricing based on the profit percentage you expect. Costs include materials, distribution, advertising, and overhead. Many experts recommend adding 25 to 50 percent to each cost estimate, especially overhead, to ensure you don't underestimate.

▶ *Distribution.* This includes the entire process of moving the product from the factory to the end user. The type of distribution network you choose depends on your industry and the size of the market. How much will it cost to reach your target market? Does that market consist of upscale customers who will pay extra for a premium product or service, or budget-conscious consumers looking for a good deal? Study your competitors to see what channels they use. Will you use the same channels or a different method that may give you a strategic advantage?

▶ *Sales.* Explain how your sales force (if you have one) will meet its goals, including elements such as pricing flexibility, sales presentations, lead generation, and compensation policies.

Competitive Analysis

How does your business relate to the competition? The competitive analysis section answers this question. Using what you've learned from your market research, detail the strengths and weaknesses of your competitors, the strategies that give you a distinct advantage, any barriers you can develop to prevent new competition from entering the market, and any weaknesses in your competitors' service or product development cycle that you can take advantage of.

The competitive analysis is an important part of your business plan. Often, startup entrepreneurs mistakenly believe their product or service is the first of its kind and fails to recognize that competition exists. In reality, every business has competition, whether direct or indirect. Your plan must show that you recognize this and have a strategy for dealing with the competition.

Design and Development Plan

This section describes a product's design and charts its development within the context of production, marketing, and the company itself. If you have an idea but have not yet developed the product or service, if you plan to improve an existing product or service, or if you own an existing company and plan to introduce a new product or service, this section is extremely important. (If your product is already completely designed and developed, you don't need to complete this section. If you are offering a service, you will need to concentrate only on the development half of the section.)

The design section should thoroughly describe the product's design and the materials used; include any diagrams if applicable. The development plan generally covers these three areas: 1) product development, 2) market development, and 3) organizational development. If you're offering a service, cover only the last two.

Create a schedule that shows how the product, marketing strategies, and organization will develop over time. The schedule should be tied to a development budget so expenses can be tracked throughout the design and development process.

Operations and Management Plan

Here, you describe how your business will function on a daily basis. This section explains logistics such as the responsibilities of each member of the management team, the tasks assigned to each division of the company (if applicable), and the capital and expense requirements for operating the business.

Describe the business's managers and their qualifications, and specify what type of support staff will be needed for the business to run efficiently. Any potential benefits or pitfalls to the community should also be presented, such as new job creation, economic growth, and possible effects on the environment from manufacturing and how they will be handled to comply with local, state, and federal regulations.

Financial Factors

The financial statements are the backbone of your business plan. They show how profitable your business will be in the short and long term, and should include the following:

▶ The income statement details the business's cash-generating ability. It projects such items as revenue, expenses, capital (in the form of depreciation), and cost of goods. You should generate a monthly income statement for the business's first year, quarterly statements for the second year, and annual statements for each year thereafter (usually for three, five, or ten years, with five being the most common).

▶ The cash flow statement details the amount of money coming into and going out of the business—monthly for the first year and quarterly for each year thereafter. The result is a profit or loss at the end of the period represented by each column. Both profits and losses carry over to the last column to show a cumulative amount. If your cash flow statement shows you consistently operating at a loss, you will probably need additional cash to meet expenses. Most businesses have some seasonal variations in their budgets, so re-examine your cash flow calculations if they look identical every month.

▶ The balance sheet paints a picture of the business's financial strength in terms of assets, liabilities, and equity over a set period. You should generate a balance sheet for each year profiled in the development of your business.

After these essential financial documents, include any relevant summary information that's not included elsewhere in the plan but will significantly affect the business. This could include ratios such as return on investment, break-even point, or return on assets. Your accountant can help you decide what information is best to include.

Many people consider the financial section of a business plan the most difficult to write. If you haven't started your business yet, how do you know what your income will be? You have a few options. The first is to enlist your accountant's help. An accountant can take your raw data and organize it into categories that will satisfy all the requirements of a financial section, including monthly and yearly sales projections. Or, if you are familiar with accounting procedures, you can do it yourself with the help of a good spreadsheet program.

Regulation and Taxation

Extraordinary federal controls on alcoholic beverages are as American as Kentucky bourbon. At first, the federal government controlled alcoholic beverages because the excise taxes on beer and booze were the country's chief source of revenue. Prohibition in 1920 ended that source of tax money. Thoroughly demonized in the process, alcoholic beverages remained the work of the devil for generations and were regulated accordingly. To this day, in certain ultraconservative corners of the country, beer, spirits, wine, and hard cider retain that sinful cache.

The craft movement is bringing alcoholic beverages out from under that shadow. Today's regulatory battles are leveling a playing field tilted in favor of large multinational producers and distribution companies with outsized control of national markets. The real financial significance of progress on taxation and regulation reform makes membership in the Brewers Association, American Craft Spirits Association, or the U.S. Association of Cider Makers one of the best business investments an independent producer can make. The craft trade associations should be your first stop when planning to enter one of these business sectors.

Washington

The craft beer pioneers and the various groups that have lobbied Congress on their behalf over the past four decades—most notably the Brewers Association (BA)—have been remarkably effective in overhauling beer regulations. Associations representing craft distillers and cider makers are gearing up for similar congressional battles. "The best possible way to get legislation changed is to get the legislators into your distillery," says Ralph Erenzo, founder of Tuthilltown Spirits in New York's Hudson Valley. "This is a traditional American craft that disappeared, but it can come back. We are going up against big brands with deep pockets, and we're trying to push them aside on a fixed store shelf."

When Erenzo goes to Washington to lobby on behalf of the American Craft Spirits Association, he tells the same story the brewers started telling 20 years ago—craft producers create local jobs and become a lure for tourists to visit often overlooked regions. He is fighting for the same tax relief and relaxed controls on distribution and sales that have been instrumental to the growth of craft beer. "The tax consideration on a federal level is what allowed craft breweries to take off," he says.

A similar tax break for craft distillers should happen. The large liquor companies "have realized we are not their enemy," he says. "We are taking all of the chances, creating the brands, and creating the market. We are their next acquisition target," which suits many craft distillers' goals. When the larger spirits industry has to fight for a new law, "we're in every state, a grassroots opportunity to transfer the image of spirits into a small business/tourism/farm support business." The problem is the craft distillers themselves. "There is a certain wildcatter's mentality. The lack of organization is a stumbling block to national regulatory reform."

Craft hard cider makers also want tax relief. To get it, they believe hard cider needs to be recognized as a distinct category separate from wine and beer, according to U.S. Association of Cider Makers president Mike Beck, owner of Michigan-based Uncle John's Cider. Today, it is regulated as wine. "Hard cider production is a direct benefit for growers. It's a local product. We need to raise the profile of hard cider in America and explain what it is."

Without the early and significant federal tax breaks for craft breweries, there might not have been a craft beer revolution. Tax relief for small spirits and hard cider producers is just as critical to the development of these sectors.

The States

The federal fight is fairly straightforward. The more difficult battles are in the states over byzantine regulations controlling distribution and sales. The political compromise necessary for Congress to pass the 21st Amendment and repeal Prohibition in 1933 gave each state the power to impose its own restrictions on production, sales, and distribution of alcoholic beverages. Some states also allow localities to gild the lily and add a layer of regulation all their own.

There is no quick way to know all of the regulations that might apply to your particular operation or to the building you plan to turn into your brewery/distillery/cider house. When shopping for a location, be aware of the local regulatory environment. There are federal/state/county/city requirements concerning the environmental impact of your operation, fire codes, water use, seismic standards, and zoning. Learn about all of the regulations governing your favorite location before you fall in love with the building. Your goal is to minimize surprises.

A hidden cost is wait time, says Ben Roesch, owner/brewer at Wormtown Brewery (http://wormtownbrewery.com), in Worcester, Massachusetts. "You are supposed to have a constructed facility before you submit your application to the Federal Alcohol and Tobacco Tax and Trade Bureau (TTB), who can take months to get back to you and then may want changes.

tip

Before starting construction, learn which government agencies will need to approve your project—planning commissions, zoning boards, neighborhood associations, the fire department, environmental review boards. Meet with their staffs. Show them detailed plans early in the process. Respond to their concerns when a change only requires a new drawing, not a new building.

You give the federal permit to the state, who may take months to approve your license. Then you make any necessary applications to your local government. All of this time you have mortgage or rent payments, equipment loans, employees to pay. And this is after you've paid tradespeople to install the equipment and had plumbers and electricians working." So, be ready to hurry up and wait. Getting through the federal and state red tape can be frustrating.

"Read your state laws before you do anything," says Erenzo. "Read them again and again until they make sense to you. Cities and counties have their zoning issues. Read those laws again and again. Then worry about the federal laws. It's complicated but, in general, the feds control production and labeling, and states control distribution and sales."

Federal Alcoholic Beverage Laws

The U.S. TTB sets the rules for the production, distribution, labeling, advertising, trade and pricing practices, credit, container characteristics, and alcoholic content of each alcoholic beverage. But, in the main, you need to focus on:

- ▶ Operating permits, label approvals, formula approvals
- ▶ Distribution
- ▶ Taxes

Before you apply for your licenses and permits, know what you want to produce (including recipes), how you want to produce it (equipment and facilities), and how you will market and label it (claims you will make to the public). These must be in final form. You need to be ready to start production with construction completed and equipment purchased and installed. That's a big capital investment to have hanging in the balance while you wait for a stranger to give you a thumbs-up. Do your homework, and don't leave anything to chance.

tip

The TTB website—ttb.gov—does a great job detailing their rules and requirements. All of their forms are readily available. The hiccup is when you need to talk to these overwhelmed civil servants or are waiting to hear back from them on a filing. TTB's budget has been slashed repeatedly during the last several congressional budget battles. And now, facing an avalanche of new applications for operating permits and approvals for formulas and labels, they are short-handed. Be prepared to wait.

"The problem with the TTB is they are underfunded and understaffed," says Erenzo. "There were ten craft distilleries in 2003, now there are 700 new distilleries with individual labels for each product to be approved. The delays are holding back the economic power of the sector."

Permits and Approvals

Breweries and distilleries report wait-times of six to eight months for operating permits, even though ttb.gov suggests things move along at a faster clip. These permits involve not just a completed application. There are background checks of you and your key employees, field investigations, equipment and premises examinations, and other paperwork requirements. Label and formula approvals are separate and seem to move along a bit faster. And make sure you meet all requirements for bond coverage by covering all aspects of your plans with your insurance agent.

Distribution

To sell products, the federally mandated three-tier distribution system requires licensed alcoholic beverage producers be separate from licensed alcoholic beverage distributors, which are separate from retailers. This was intended to end the practice of producer-owned retailers, which were considered anti-competitive.

Today, it seems an archaic and inefficient system that imposes undue burdens on small producers while giving excessive power to distributors. These state-based businesses have merged into national distribution giants with enormous power. Southern Wine & Spirits (www. southernwine.com), the largest of these distribution giants, dominates alcoholic beverage distribution throughout much of the country. While producers set their own prices, distributors are the gatekeepers to the market and have enormous influence on how various products are sold and at what price.

Taxes

There are separate federal tax rates for each of the three craft alcoholic beverage categories. Whatever happens, do not fail to pay your federal taxes on time and in full. The

aha!

The counterbalance to the big distributors is the emergence of new craft-oriented distributors who are creating a parallel distribution track separate from the giant distributors to meet the demand for craft beverages. The opportunity for these new distributors is growing with the rise of craft. Consider hitching a ride to their stars.

"revenue man" DNA is still in the federal alcoholic beverage bureaucracy. They pay careful attention to tax receipts. Pay the Taxman, or he will surely shut you down.

Craft brewers making less than two million barrels of beer a year pay federal excise taxes of $7 per barrel (31 gallons) on the first 60,000 barrels they brew. They pay $18 per barrel on every barrel thereafter, which is the tax rate for larger breweries. So far the only craft brewer to outgrow this federal tax break is Boston Beer. The BA is lobbying for an even deeper tax break for very small breweries, and a slightly lower rate for midsize craft breweries.

Craft distillers receive no federal tax break and pay the same $13.50 per proof gallon (100 proof or 50 percent alcohol), or $4 per each 750 ml bottle paid by Diageo and Pernod-Ricard. New York Senator Charles Schumer and others in Congress are pushing legislation to lower the tax rate for craft distillers in a scheme similar to what craft brewers enjoy. Their argument casts craft distillers as job creators, bringing tourism to underpopulated areas, the same argument that worked so well for craft breweries.

By federal law, hard cider must be made primarily of apple juice and, in most instances, is treated like wine, taxed at a rate of $0.21 per 750 ml bottle or $1.07/gallon if less than 14 percent alcohol. But hard cider is naturally fizzy, which moves many artisan ciders into the "naturally sparkling" category, which is taxed at a rate three-times higher: $0.67 per 750 ml bottle or $3.40/gal. In some cases, depending on a technical analysis of the hard cider, a lower rate may be available for small cider houses. Confusion over which tax rate applies can be costly.

Once again, my friends at Entrepreneur are going to jump in here and fill you in on the details of an essential start-up function--hiring an accountant. They will cover what to look for in an accountant, dos and don'ts of hiring one, and how much to pay for their services.

Hiring an Accountant

You want to spend your time brewing the best beer, distilling the finest spirits, or pressing the purest cider. That's why it is a good idea to hire out the numbers help. Don't assume only big companies need the services of an accountant. Accountants help you keep an eye on major costs as early as the startup stage, a time when you're probably preoccupied with counting every paper clip and postage stamp. Accountants help you look at the big picture.

Even after the startup stage, many business owners may not have any idea how well they're doing financially until the end of the year, when they file their tax returns. Meanwhile, they equate their cash flow with profits, which is wrong. Every dollar counts for business owners, so if you don't know where you stand on a monthly basis, you may not be around at the end of the year.

While do-it-yourself accounting software is plentiful and easy to use, it's not the sole answer. Just as having Microsoft Word does not make you a writer, having accounting software doesn't make you an accountant. Software can only do what you tell it to do—and a good accountant's skills go far beyond crunching numbers.

In fact, perhaps no other business relationship has such potential to pay off. Nowadays, accountants are more than just bean counters. A good accountant can be your company's financial partner for life—with intimate knowledge of everything from how you're going to finance your next forklift to how you're going to finance your daughter's college education.

While many people think of accountants strictly as tax preparers, in reality, accountants have a wide knowledge base that can be an invaluable asset to a business. A general accounting practice covers four basic areas of expertise:

1. Business advisory services
2. Accounting and record-keeping
3. Tax advice
4. Auditing

These four disciplines often overlap. For instance, if your accountant is helping you prepare the financial statements you need for a loan, and he or she gives you some insights into how certain estimates could be recalculated to get a more favorable review, the accountant is crossing the line from auditing into business advisory services. And perhaps, after preparing your midyear financial statements, he or she might suggest how your performance year-to-date will influence your year-end tax liability. Here's a closer look at the four areas:

1. *Business advisory services.* This is where accountants can really earn their keep. Since the accountant is knowledgeable about your business environment, your tax situation, and your financial statements, it makes sense to ask him or her to pull all the pieces together and help you come up with a business plan and personal financial plan you can really achieve. Accountants can offer advice on everything from insurance (do you really need business interruption insurance, or would it be cheaper to lease a second site?) to expansion (how will additional capacity affect operating costs?). Accountants can bring a new level of insight to the picture, simply by virtue of their perspective.

2. *Accounting and record-keeping.* Accounting and record-keeping are perhaps the most basic accounting discipline. However, most business owners keep their own books and records instead of having their accountant do it. The reason is simple: If

these records are examined by lenders or the IRS, the business owner is responsible for their accuracy; therefore, it makes more sense for the owner to maintain them.

Where accountants can offer help is in initially setting up bookkeeping and accounting systems and showing the business owner how to use them. A good system allows you to evaluate your profitability at any given point in time and modify prices accordingly. It also lets you track expenses to see if any particular areas are getting out of hand. It lets you establish and track a budget, spot trends in sales and expenses, and reduce accounting fees required to produce financial statements and tax returns.

3. *Tax advice.* Tax help from accountants comes in two forms: tax compliance and tax planning. Planning refers to reducing your overall tax burden; compliance refers to obeying the tax laws.

4. *Auditing.* Auditing services are required for many different purposes, most commonly by banks as a condition of a loan. There are many levels of auditing, ranging from simply preparing financial statements from figures that you supply all the way up to an actual audit, where the accountant or other third party gives assurance that a company's financial information is accurate.

Choosing an Accountant

The best way to find a good accountant is to get a referral from your attorney, your banker, or a business colleague in the same industry. If you need more possibilities, almost every state has a Society of Certified Public Accountants that will make a referral. Don't underestimate the importance of a CPA. This title is only awarded to people who have passed a rigorous two-day, nationally standardized test. Most states require CPAs to have at least a college degree or its equivalent, and several states also require post-graduate work.

Accountants usually work for large companies; CPAs, on the other hand, work for a variety of large and small businesses. When dealing with an accountant, you can only hope he or she is well-educated and well-versed in your business's needs. Passing the CPA exam, however, is a guarantee of a certain level of ability. Once you have come up with some good candidates, a little preparation is in order before you interview them. The first step in setting the stage for a successful search is to take an inventory of what you will need. It is important to determine beforehand just how much of the work your company will do and how much of it will be done by the accountant.

Accounting services can be broken down into three broad categories: recording transactions, assembling them, and generating returns and financial statements. Typically, the latter part—that is, the generation of returns and financial statements—requires the highest level of expertise. But though the other activities require a lower skill level, many firms still charge the same hourly rate for them. Given the level of fees you are prepared to pay, you must decide where your responsibility stops and where the accountant's begins.

Once you have compiled your documentation and given some thought to your expectations, you're ready to interview your referrals. Five candidates is a good number to start with. For each candidate, plan on two meetings before making your decision. One of these meetings should be at your site; one should be at theirs. Both parties need to know the environment the other works in. Your principal goal is to find out about three things: services, personality, and fees.

1. *Services.* Most accounting firms offer tax and auditing services. But what about bookkeeping? Management consulting? Pension fund accounting? Estate planning? Will the accountant help you design and implement financial information systems? Other services a CPA may offer include analyzing transactions for loans and financing; preparing, auditing, reviewing, and compiling financial statements; managing investments; and representing you before tax authorities.

    Although smaller accounting firms are generally a better bet for entrepreneurs, they may not offer all these services. Make sure the firm has what you need. If it can't offer specialized services, such as estate planning, it may have relationships with other firms to which it can refer you to handle these matters. In addition to services, make sure the firm has experience with small business and with your industry. Someone who is already familiar with the financial issues facing your particular avenue of the craft industry won't have to waste time getting up to speed.

2. *Personality.* Is the accountant's style compatible with yours? Be sure the people you are meeting with are the same ones who will be handling your business. At many accounting firms, some partners handle sales and new business, then pass the actual account work on to others.

    When evaluating competency and compatibility, ask candidates how they would handle situations relevant to you. For example: How would you handle a change in corporation status from S to C? How would you handle an IRS office audit seeking verification of automobile expenses? Listen to the answers, and decide if that's how you would like your affairs to be handled.

    Realize, too, that having an accountant who takes a different approach can be a good thing. If you are super conservative, it's not a bad thing to have an accountant who exposes you to the aggressive side of life. Likewise, if you are aggressive, it's often helpful to have someone who can show you the conservative approach. Be sure that the accountant won't pressure you into doing things you aren't comfortable with. You need to be able to sleep at night.

3. *Fees*. Ask about fees upfront. Most accounting firms charge by the hour; fees can range from $100 to $275 per hour. However, there are some accountants who work on a monthly retainer. Figure out what services you are likely to need and which option will be more cost-effective for you.

Get a range of quotes from different accountants. Also try to get an estimate of the total annual charges based on the services you have discussed. Don't base your decision solely on cost, however; an accountant who charges more by the hour is likely to be more experienced and thus able to work faster than a novice who charges less.

At the end of the interview, ask for references—particularly from clients in the same industry as you. A good accountant should be happy to provide you with references; call and ask how satisfied they were with the accountant's services, fees, and availability.

Finding and hiring a reputable accountant will save you considerable money in the long run.

State Alcoholic Beverage Laws

Just when you think the financial and regulatory fun is more than you can handle, here come the alcoholic beverage laws! Lest you think there is just one set of laws, each of the 50 states and the District of Columbia has its own distinct set of rules for each kind of alcoholic beverage.

With the repeal of Prohibition, the federal government got out of the business of regulating alcohol distribution and gave it to the states. The resulting state-specific regulations means a production facility may meet the requirements of its home state, yet fall short of the requirements necessary to sell products in the state next door. It is often easier to sell products overseas than it is to sell to another state. Below, we've detailed a few states and the ways in which they do business to show you just how diverse the business environment can be for the craft industry. See Figure 4–1 on page 59 for more information on craft beer in each state.

Texas

"We still had Prohibition marketing laws [in Texas] when we opened in 1994," says Brock Wagner, founder of Saint Arnold Brewing Company (www.saintarnold.com) in Houston. "You could not have a pre-arranged promotion at a bar or restaurant. You could have a

Rank	Brewing Company	City	State
1	D. G. Yuengling and Son, Inc	Pottsville	PA
2	Boston Beer Co	Boston	MA
3	Sierra Nevada Brewing Co	Chico	CA
4	New Belgium Brewing Co	Fort Collins	CO
5	Gambrinus	Shiner	TX
6	Lagunitas Brewing Co	Petaluma	CA
7	Bell's Brewery, Inc	Galesburg	MI
8	Deschutes Brewery	Bend	OR
9	Stone Brewing Co	Escondido	CA
10	Minhas Craft Brewery	Monroe	WI
11	Brooklyn Brewery	Brooklyn	NY
12	Duvel Moortgat USA	Kansas City & Cooperstown	MO/NY
13	Dogfish Head Craft Brewery	Milton	DE
14	Matt Brewing Co	Utica	NY
15	Harpoon Brewery	Boston	MA
16	Firestone Walker Brewing Co	Paso Robles	CA
17	Founders Brewing Co	Grand Rapids	MI
18	SweetWater Brewing Co	Atlanta	GA
19	New Glarus Brewing Co	New Glarus	WI
20	Alaskan Brewing Co	Juneau	AK
21	Abita Brewing Co	Abita Springs	LA
22	Anchor Brewing Co	San Francisco	CA
23	Great Lakes Brewing Co	Cleveland	OH
24	Oskar Blues Brewery	Longmont	CO
25	Shipyard Brewing Co	Portland	ME
26	Stevens Point Brewery Co	Stevens Point	WI
27	August Schell Brewing Co	New Ulm	MN
28	Summit Brewing Co	Saint Paul	MN
29	Victory Brewing Co	Downingtown	PA
30	Long Trail Brewing Co	Bridgewater Corners	VT

FIGURE 4–1: **Top 50 U.S. Craft Brewing Companies**
(Based on 2014 beer sales volume) *Credit*: Brewers Association

Rank	Brewing Company	City	State
31	Ballast Point Brewing & Spirits	San Diego	CA
32	Rogue Ales Brewery & Headquarters	Newport	OR
33	Full Sail Brewing Co	Hood River	OR
34	Odell Brewing Co	Fort Collins	CO
35	Southern Tier Brewing Co	Lakewood	NY
36	Ninkasi Brewing Co	Eugene	OR
37	Flying Dog Brewery	Frederick	MD
38	Uinta Brewing Co	Salt Lake City	UT
39	Bear Republic Brewing Co	Cloverdale	CA
40	Left Hand Brewing Company	Longmont	CO
41	21st Amendment Brewery Cafe	San Francisco	CA
42	Allagash Brewing Co	Portland	ME
43	Lost Coast Brewery and Cafe	Eureka	CA
44	Troegs Brewing Co	Hershey	PA
45	Karl Strauss Brewing Co	San Diego	CA
46	Saint Arnold Brewing Co	Houston	TX
47	Narragansett Brewing Co	Providence	RI
48	Green Flash Brewing Co	San Diego	CA
49	Craftworks Restaurants & Breweries, Inc	Chattanooga & Louisville	TN/ CO
50	Breckenridge Brewery	Denver	CO

FIGURE 4–1: **Top 50 U.S. Craft Brewing Companies,** continued
(Based on 2014 beer sales volume) *Credit*: Brewers Association

promotion, but you couldn't tell anyone you were going to have it. It was like throwing a party without inviting anyone," says Wagner. "If you opened a brewery, you couldn't sell beer there. Taprooms are critical for a small brewery to survive.

"The legislature was in the pocket of the beer wholesalers. Mike McKinney was the evil player. [As head of the state association representing the beer distributors] he was the most powerful lobbyist in Texas. He had money and he threw it around. Politicians told me, 'We love you but the wholesalers give us too much money. We can't help you.'

He passed away a couple of years ago. We got the taproom law changed this year," in 2014.

"The beer wholesalers are some of the wealthiest people in the country. One hundred percent of the alcohol in this country goes through their hands. Texas has thousands of alcoholic beverage suppliers, and thousands of retailers, and two or three [distributors] get a 25 percent cut of everything sold. Texas regulators acted as a collection agency for the distributors. You bounce a check to a distributor, the Texas Alcoholic Beverage Commission came after you," said Wagner.

Ron Extract, founder of Jester King Brewery (http://jesterkingbrewery.com) in Austin, adds, "A lot of work still needs to be done to make Texas competitive with the rest of the country. But it's gotten better. When we started four years ago, there were only 25 breweries in Texas. Now there are more than 100 and lots more are planned."

In general, direct sales, brewery tours, brewpubs, microbreweries, excise taxes, packaging, and franchising regulations are more stringent throughout the southern half of the country. While craft producers are as likely to be Republicans as Democrats, progressive states have been more willing to roll back Prohibition-era laws, even when those rollbacks upset the interests of companies reliant on those established regulatory hierarchies. New York State is among the most aggressive states in this regard.

New York State

Undoubtedly, New York is the most craft-friendly state. Each year for the last four years, Governor Andrew Cuomo has taken further steps to support the state's craft breweries, distilleries, cideries, and wineries. He has made on-site sales of both by-the-glass and packaged goods legal, simplified or eliminated state permitting, enacted tax cuts; abolished bond requirements, and provided grants for marketing support and self-distribution. The goal is to foster small business development and help the state recover from the recession. New York craft producers who source at least 51 percent of their ingredients in-state are the big winners. "They leap-frogged everyone," says Rodewald. "It's smart. They don't have an industrial liquor industry, and they elevated their local grain and produce production out of the commodity market."

"Within the liquor industry there is enormous opportunity for growth with the explosive interest in local products," says New York State Liquor Authority chairman Dennis Rosen. "There are now some very big beer companies that started out very small. We are doing this to grow the industry and employ a lot of people, which is a wonderful thing. It's not that New Yorkers are drinking more. We are cutting into the global companies' share of the market." New York State producers employing New York State residents are creating goods that supplant products produced in other countries. "The vibrations of that are felt down the line in wide-ranging ways," he says.

"With things like self-distribution, we've carved out exemptions to the three-tier system for small producers. Generally, those tiers have to be independent of each other. We can't extend the exemptions too far without getting sued for violating the commerce clause." At this point, Rosen says the state has gone as far as it believes it can to support craft producers. The push back from large producers and distributors, he says, has become significant.

Rosen's next step is to try to clarify New York's alcoholic beverage laws. "We are operating with laws that were written as the nation was coming out of Prohibition. There are rules that don't seem to make sense now. Everyone complains that the laws are anachronistic. One of the things very disappointing to me as we work on a top-to-bottom revision is that the larger interests oppose what we're doing. No matter how flawed the system, it works well for them."

New York's holistic approach to nurturing the craft sector is having an impact. Between 2011 and 2014, the number of New York microbreweries increased 175 percent to 109 breweries; brewpubs increased 230 percent to 33; cider producers increased five-fold to 28; farm distilleries increased from 10 to 51; other small distilleries increased 164 percent to 37. There are 70 new farm breweries since that license was approved in 2012. Rosen points to New York City residents' new awareness of the rest of the state and support for what's happening outside the city as a positive result.

This progressive approach to supporting craft is spreading, particularly in the area of self-distribution and direct sales. Small breweries, distilleries and cider houses in more and more states are able to sell directly to customers, not just in their taprooms, but also by delivering kegs and packaged goods to restaurants and convenience stores. Even in Utah, which historically has had regressive alcoholic beverage laws, Park City's High West Distillery (www.highwest.com) sells bottles of its Rendezvous Rye in its distillery store and serves drinks at a bar in the distillery.

States you would expect to be on the forefront of regulatory change, such as California, have been slower to buck entrenched alcoholic beverage companies.

California

In California, spirits producers are gearing up to fight for a New York-style regulatory overhaul. Currently, they are limited to selling a thimbleful of a maximum of six different products to distillery visitors. "We need to be able to sell from our distillery tasting room. It is the only

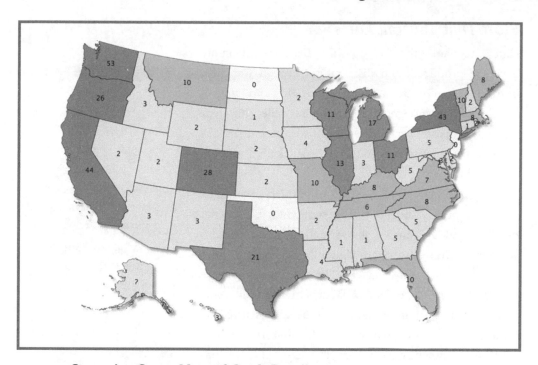

FIGURE 4–2: **State-by-State Map of Craft Distilleries**

way to tell your story to consumers and know that they understand what you are doing," says Cris Steller, executive director of the California Artisanal Distillers Guild and founder of Dry Diggings Distillery (www.drydiggingsdistillery.com) in El Dorado, California.

"Distributors are fighting back hard. California is one of the top five markets for spirits in the world, and they think they are going to give up market share if we can sell out of our distilleries. They cast it as 'holding the line against demon booze.' But when Utah looks progressive, you know you are behind. New York, Colorado, Washington, Oregon all leapfrogged us. California is down at the bottom with Alabama and Kansas," says Steller, noting that when he lobbied Governor Jerry Brown on the issue, "he didn't even know about the rules and called it 'ridiculous.' We'll have this in another year."

"There is no easy money in distilling," he says. "What I'm doing makes no sense as a business. It's hard work, time, effort, and luck. The industry is driven by bartenders and mixologists. If someone is going to pay me what my bourbon costs to make, they are going to want to meet me, come to my distillery, and taste it with me and ask lots of questions. People will spend the money. They just want to know why it is worth it." See Figure 4–2 for a look at the country's full range of craft distilleries.

State Distribution Laws

States regulate the relationship between alcoholic beverage producers and distributors through franchise laws. You can enter a franchise relationship with a simple verbal agreement to move a single shipment through a distributor. But if your distributor turns out to be a disappointment, you may be stuck in a loveless relationship.

Franchise laws were designed to correct a perceived imbalance in bargaining power between powerful, national brewers, and the smaller state-specific wholesalers who serve them. In reality, consolidation has made both sides of that equation evenly balanced. The mice in the room are craft producers. Cancellations, failures to renew, attempts to modify a distribution agreement are all restricted by franchise laws written to protect the distributor.

Worse, franchise laws vary by state. The BA has created a database of U.S. beer franchise laws governing beer sales in each state. Before entering a contract with a wholesaler, learn how specific states regulate this relationship because state laws may trump contract terms. With spirits, there are two types of state regulatory environments. Open states allow alcoholic beverages to be sold through private entities; control states sell through state liquor control boards. State franchise laws trump distribution contracts for spirits in open states just as they do for beer.

Eugene Pak, an attorney with the law firm of Wendel, Rosen, Black & Dean specializing in brewery law, suggests getting professional help before entering any distribution arrangements. Mistakes here are critical. "Set a term for your distribution agreements to expire. Most states prohibit termination without cause," he says. And if they do allow you to walk away from an unhappy relationship, you will pay dearly—one to five times your net profits.

> **tip**
>
> Keep your eye on the horizon when it comes to alternate formats for sales and shipping. Brick-and-mortar locations are the heart of the craft business, but many businesses are trading on a savvy online buyers' market as well. The next regulatory hurdle? "Internet sales and direct shipments to customers will be huge," Pak told the group. "Things are changing fast to make this happen."

State Taxes

There is great disparity and volatility in state taxation rates. For beer, Tennessee has had the highest state excise tax at $1.17 per gallon followed by Florida and Georgia at 48 cents per gallon. Wyoming has the lowest at two cents per gallon. The U.S. average rate is about 19 cents per gallon.

▶ Be Careful What You Ask For

There were no craft breweries in Springfield, Illinois, in 2010, when Chris Trudeau graduated from design school and convinced his mom they should work together and build one on the family farm near the city. Trudeau's high school friend and his mom joined up to make it a team of four at Rolling Meadows Brewery (http://rollingmeadowsbrewery.com). After a course in beer making at Chicago's Siebel Institute of Technology and then some classes at the University of California at Davis in their legendary brewery program, they drafted plans to build a seven-barrel brewery using the farm's soft red wheat and wild hops.

As they were designing the new brewery, Anheuser-Busch In-Bev sued Illinois claiming Illinois' small brewer exemption to the three-tier system was "thinly veiled economic protectionism" favoring in-state brewers and a violation of the Commerce Clause inhibiting interstate commerce. "Basically, Anheuser-Busch was trying to take away our right to self-distribute. They didn't like the fact that Illinois craft brewers were allowed to sell directly to taverns and retailers while out-of-state brewers, like themselves, had to use a middleman," says Trudeau. "If Rolling Meadows had to pay a distributor, it would have messed up our whole business plan. We thought we would have to sell our brewery equipment or switch to making soda. Then we decided to push back."

Once the suit was filed, the judge stopped all self-distribution and asked the state legislature to take up the issue. "I was crapping my pants. We're depending on the dysfunctional Illinois state government to do something quickly? I called my state representative, Rich Brauer. He asked me how much beer I made. I told him we make 15,000 barrels a year and self-distribute half of that," Trudeau says, taking a stab at what those numbers would be if they ever got a chance to build the brewery then sitting in boxes.

"Suddenly I became a lobbyist, competing head-on with Budweiser's lobbyists and the big distributors' lobbyists, all people I had no intention of ever tangling with. I showed up for a hearing on the bill at the Capitol wearing a T-shirt and jeans with my hair all disheveled because I rushed over on my bike. I told them I just want my small family brewery to bring around a little beer to a few establishments and that at some point I would want to work with a distributor.

"Then the media gets ahold of the story and all of these people start calling their representatives and the bill passes and is signed by the governor. The new law enacted June 2011 permits breweries that produce 15,000 barrels or less a year to self-distribute up to 7,500 barrels."

State and local excise taxes on spirits are equally random. The taxes can include fixed-rate per volume taxes; wholesale taxes that are usually a percentage of the value of the product; distributor taxes (usually structured as license fees but are often a percentage of revenues); retail taxes, in which retailers owe an extra percentage of revenues; case or bottle fees (which can vary based on size of container); and additional sales taxes (note that this measure does not include general sales tax, only those in excess of the general rate). In other words, always check with your state tax authority first—and don't count on continuity.

Craft Businesses That Work

Craft producers crave independence and freedom. Opening a craft brewery, distillery, or cidery usually involves partnering with friends or family who share your vision. As businesses mature, financial needs lead to more complex business arrangements. But during the current "neighborhood" age of the craft movement, when the best opportunities for new ventures are often the ones that start in an abandoned building down the road from where you live, working with a partner, in whatever kind of form it takes, makes life easier.

If partners stick together through the difficult years, sharing the burdens enhances a startup's chances. The challenge is setting the partnership up to reward each individual's sweat equity. "I've spent 20 years marketing Firestone Walker. What is the value you would put on that chunk of your life?" asks David Walker, cofounder of Firestone Walker Brewery Company (www.firestonebeer.com) with brother-in-law Adam Firestone.

Twenty years, says Walker, is the minimum planning horizon for a new brewery. "Don't start if you have to make it work in five years." Launched in 1996, during the deadly lull in the craft beer business, Firestone Walker was located in the Santa Barbara wine region, physically cut off from California's beer revolution. "It was a dark time," he says. The partners relocated two hours north to Paso Robles in 2002 and built a pub next to their production brewery. But the struggle continued with sales topping out at 50,000 barrels in 2006.

tip

Firestone Walker's David Walker says that, these days, you can start your craft business on a shoestring. "Everyone near you, including Whole Foods, will carry your beer. Once you get to the next level—around 15,000 barrels/year—marketing and distribution are very expensive. It will be 25 percent of your budget. The window for expanding from microbrewery status to be a regional brewery is closing. You may be stuck on that 15,000 barrel plateau," he says, so be prepared to adjust accordingly. Most importantly Walker says, "Whoever gives you money for investment can cause havoc. Make sure they are aligned with your long-term vision."

▶ Risky Business

There are risks. Two well-written tales of building a craft brewery—Sam Calagione's *Brewing Up a Business: Adventures in Beer from the Founder of Dogfish Head Craft Brewery* (John Wiley & Sons, 2011) and Ken Grossman's *Beyond the Pale: The Story of Sierra Nevada Brewing Co.* (John Wiley & Sons, 2013)—detail the painful and nearly fatal fallout of failed partnerships. Tony Magee's *So You Want to Start a Brewery?: The Lagunitas Story* (Chicago Review Press, 2014) details the intense pressure and daily challenges of running a one-man show in the craft alcoholic beverage business. Make them a part of your required startup reading.

When the market finally woke up to their distinctive oak-barrel fermented ales, it took them by surprise. Firestone Walker sold 200,000 barrels of beer in 2014 with sales growing 45 percent annually. With a second brewery opening in Los Angeles in 2015, near the beach in Venice, Walker expects sales to be twice that by 2016. They are now one of the top 20 craft breweries in the country. "I'm a little confused by it all, but very happy."

Walker's advice for new craft brewers is simple: "Focus on making extraordinary beers. Narrow your geographic expectations. Beer performs best near the brewery. Think big within a small footprint. Value your product and don't discount. We expect some ugly price wars with so much new competition; avoid them at all costs."

Before planning how you will market your business, "listen to people's stories," says Charlie Papazian, president of the Brewer Association. "This is a unique industry. Before you spend any money, spend your time learning the technology, science, and art. Gobble up all the information you can. This is a highly regulated business, and you need to understand it. Go to conferences."

Remember to:

▶ Protect personal assets by separating them from business liabilities through an LLC, corporation, or partnership early in the development of the business. The more formal the documentation (e.g., partnership or LLC agreement), the better.

▶ Take care with potential investors. Selling shares in a craft venture involves registering or at least filing with the Securities and Exchange Commission as well as the state where the business is registered. In general, you cannot widely advertise that you are selling shares, and there are laws governing your communications with potential investors.

▶ Protect intellectual property, particularly trademarks, by registering them as soon as possible with the U.S. Patent and Trademark Office. Reserve your internet domain names promptly.

▶ Hire a professional accountant to maintain accurate records of everything that happens in the business and supervise payroll.

Location, Location, Location

The craft movement is stronger in some states than others. Texas, Florida, and the Deep South, along with the middle-middle of the country—Kansas, Oklahoma, Arkansas, Nebraska, and Iowa—are far behind the rest of the country in the number of craft alcoholic beverage enterprises. Portland would seem to be a saturated market with as much as 50 percent of the beer sold there produced in the state. Ashville is leading North Carolina's craft explosion. And Washington, DC, is only just getting started.

Breweries per Capita (per 100,000 21+ adults)	State	Number of Craft Breweries	Production in Barrels	Rank by Production
1	Oregon	181	877,891	5
2	Vermont	29	229,062	16
3	Montana	39	133,465	23
4	Colorado	175	1,413,242	3
5	Maine	47	259,654	15
6	Wyoming	18	15,863	46
7	Alaska	22	182,530	20
8	Washington	201	333,175	11
9	Idaho	34	43,073	37
10	New Hampshire	22	69,164	30
11	Wisconsin	90	444,311	9
12	New Mexico	31	58,247	31
13	Washington, DC	9	14,889	47
14	Michigan	131	582,909	8
15	Iowa	40	29,417	40
16	South Dakota	10	4,008	50
17	Nebraska	22	24,467	42
18	Delaware	10	211,280	17
19	California	381	2,948,895	1
20	Indiana	63	120,828	27
21	Minnesota	52	367,681	10
22	North Carolina	91	263,488	14
23	North Dakota	6	1,866	51
24	Massachusetts	57	329,412	12
25	Pennsylvania	108	1,788,556	2
26	New York	165	859,535	6

FIGURE 5–1: **State-by-State Rankings of Craft Breweries per Capita**

Credit: Brewers Association

Breweries per Capita (per 100,000 21+ adults)	State	Number of Craft Breweries	Production in Barrels	Rank by Production
27	Missouri	49	299,214	13
28	Nevada	22	46,729	36
29	Rhode Island	8	12,218	48
30	Virginia	61	129,103	26
31	Arizona	47	117,457	28
32	Kansas	20	33,051	38
33	Ohio	76	1,097,955	4
34	Illinois	83	136,999	22
35	Connecticut	23	51,457	33
36	Utah	16	130,790	24
37	Maryland	34	171,470	21
38	Hawaii	8	25,082	41
39	Tennessee	35	98,508	29
40	Arkansas	13	10,417	49
41	South Carolina	20	46,900	35
42	Texas	96	840,259	7
43	West Virginia	7	19,542	44
44	Oklahoma	13	21,029	43
45	Kentucky	15	52,639	32
46	Florida	66	129,946	25
47	Georgia	28	207,257	18
48	New Jersey	26	48,996	34
49	Alabama	13	32,531	39
50	Louisiana	11	184,577	19
51	Mississippi	4	17,560	45

FIGURE 5–1: **State-by-State Rankings of Craft Breweries per Capita,** continued
Credit: Brewers Association

Some states do more to promote craft businesses and some states go out of their way to inhibit their growth. Opportunities exist in each of these situations. But as James Fallows wrote in the November 2014 issue of *The Atlantic*, "The presence of craft brewers—and their more hip counterparts, craft distillers—are important markers of cities that are attracting the young and ambitious." At this point, every state wants to have craft beer, spirits, and cider producers.

Florida

Florida is the third largest beer market in the country but one of the slowest to develop craft breweries. "We're a vacation market," says Mike Halker, president of Florida Brewers Guild (http://floridabrewersguild.org). "Our distributor network was entrenched, and they controlled the market. They spent lots of money to have friends in Tallahassee [the state capital]. We're a rare place where Anheuser-Busch and MillerCoors still command 95 percent of the beer market. Our consumers didn't know they wanted something that they didn't know exists." When Sam Adams and Sierra Nevada beers became available, it changed everything. Once consumers knew not everything tastes like Budweiser, they wanted more of it, he says.

"The inflection point for us was five years ago," says Halker. Twenty-five new breweries opened last year for a total of 100 craft breweries in the state. "We continue to add two a month, which is still a small number. San Diego county has more breweries than all of Florida. When the national craft brands come in, they create customers for us. So it's OK, as long as they don't slash prices. New Belgium launched in Florida with discounts. It cuts our throats."

Portland, Oregon

Marcus Reed, an attorney with Miller Nash LLP in Portland, Oregon, who specializes in representing craft breweries, says there is plenty of room for more breweries in Portland, particularly if they are neighborhood-focused and serve food. "New restaurant pubs do really well. The margins for beer sold in a brewpub are stunning. You can make the beer for 50 cents and sell it for $5 a glass. It's an order of magnitude better than selling to a distributor. The volume you can produce is limited, but you can always open another pub.

"It is getting harder for production breweries. Distributors are flooded with accounts. Store shelves are filling up. There is a limit to the number of tap handles in bars. But bars keep adding more taps, and grocery stores are adding more coolers and racks. There is opportunity if a brewery is creative.

"We are not seeing any breweries fail. There is a growing trend of new people who have very, very little experience. They are asking for trouble by having substandard quality. Still, we hesitate to discourage them. We have seen too many people succeed who we thought couldn't. We just encourage them to go work in someone else's brewery before they open their own. In Portland, every neighborhood will have a brewpub. And some will have five or six of them within walking distance of each other. We're heading for one brewery for every 5,000 people, pretty crazy. There is no sign of a slowdown. Every brewer is expanding because they have reached their maximum capacity."

"There are 70 breweries in Portland," says David Fleming, a Portland-based brewery consultant, and that doesn't count across the river in Vancouver. "I've worked for 11 of them. I see a lot of homebrewers open brewpubs. It's like a kid learning to drive a car and then getting into an 18-wheeler. They learn things the hard way. So many people I think shouldn't go forward, do it anyway and they succeed. I don't judge anyone."

Los Angeles, California

California is literally the birthplace of craft beer, says Tom McCormick, of the California Craft Brewers Association (www.californiacraftbeer.com). But throughout the revolution and until the late 1990s, most of the craft breweries were in Northern California. "San Diego happened in the late 1990s. Stone Brewery pushed that forward, and now there are 100 breweries in San Diego alone. Los Angeles was the late-bloomer and is still late to the party."

"[Los Angeles] is the largest import beer market in the country," says David Walker with Firestone Walker Brewing Company . "It imports its craft beers from Mexico. It's only 5 percent of the beer market, similar to Florida. In San Francisco, craft is 25 percent of the market. Los Angeles is neither homogeneous nor provincial, which is where craft beer took off first.

"Part of the problem is the Los Angeles city planners don't get craft beer," says Walker. "They have no idea what it is and how to cultivate it." But Los Angeles is finally starting to change. There are pockets—Downtown, Silver Lake—switching to craft. Opening a brewery in Venice, California, Walker is betting Los Angeles will transform over the next five years and become a craft city.

Golden Road is a new Los Angeles brewery, and it is starting bigger than nearly any craft brewery ever before. "Almost every brewery that has ever started big has failed," says McCormick. "That probably won't happen anymore. Golden Road is one of the new models."

warning

Choose your message carefully, and be wary of diversifying your vision. If you want to offer a taproom, do it simply and with focus. Don't delve into offering a restaurant feature if you don't have the street cred (and funding) to back it up. "I am amazed that all these brewpubs stay open," **says** David Fleming, a Portland-based brewery consultant. "I don't know where the money comes from. I keep waiting for it to drop off, but it never does."

Starting with an 80,000-barrel capacity production brewery, Tony Yanow and Meg Gill have declared Golden Road Brewing (www.goldenroad.la) to be L.A.'s brewery. "We needed a big plant for a big city. No one was even selling craft beer in Los Angeles," says Yanow. "We saw the window of opportunity closing. Someone was going to do it. We had to get up and running quickly." When they opened in 2011, there were three breweries in Los Angeles. By the end of 2014, Los Angeles had 26 breweries and 30 in development.

Hand-Crafted Companies

Craft companies are as handcrafted as their products, reflecting their founders' personalities. You want to create a company that reflects who you are and your values. But it helps to learn lessons from others who are still in business. Below are several short profiles of companies showing various approaches to operating a craft business. In the craft tradition, these founders are open about their successes and their mistakes. They hope their tips are useful. Consider them your craft business Sherpas, ready to guide you to the mountaintop.

Grand Traverse Distillery, Traverse City, Michigan
Kent Rabish, Owner
Founded 2007

"I had never had a business class or read a P&L statement before we started our distillery," says Kent Rabish, who in 2007 opened Grand Traverse Distillery (www.grandtraversedistillery. com) with his wife and son. Aside from a visit to Bend Distillery, an Oregon grain-to-glass operation, he was just as clueless about the spirits business. But that didn't bother him. After 25 years of peddling pharmaceuticals, he says, "I was bored to death."

Keeping his day job and distilling on weekends, Rabish started out the hard way—distilling from wheat, rye, and corn grown on a farm nine miles down the road. Still, within three months of firing up his shiny copper stills, his first product, True North Vodka was in all the major Michigan chain stores, a total of 1,200 accounts. First-year sales totaled $400,000; year-two sales were $800,000; year-three sales reached $1 million, and Grand Traverse Distillery turned a profit. Rabish quit selling pharmaceuticals to focus on spirits, even though it would be another two years before he could pay himself a salary. In 2014, sales reached $1.8 million.

An initial smart move, he says, was connecting with German equipment maker Arnold Holstein, who sold him a turnkey distillery with both a pot and rectifying column stills, 6,000 pounds of copper in all. The best part of this Ferrari was the distiller sent along to train Rabish and his son how to use it. The still, and related equipment, accounts for roughly two-thirds of his $1 million in capital costs. The distillery building is the rest. Rabish spent $400,000 of his and his wife's savings and borrowed the rest from a bank.

A bottle of his True North Vodka retails for $29.99, for which he is paid between roughly $14 or $16, depending on the distributor. Out of that he pays taxes—$2.14 for vodka and $2.80 for whiskey. Overhead is $4.60 per bottle. Bottles, labels, corks, caps, and packaging cost $3 per bottle. After ingredients and other costs, he makes roughly $5 a bottle.

The problem with vodka, says Rabish, is the understandable perception that all vodkas taste the same. Most commercial vodkas are distilled by a handful of industrial giants, including Cargill and Archer Daniels Midland, so they actually are the same product. "The big guys sell to the little guys, and all the little guys do is filter it and perhaps one pass of distilling. It's all from corn because, pound for pound, you get more alcohol from corn. And vodka from corn has no flavor at all," he says. "I'm Polish. I like rye vodka."

Rabish now is scrambling to shift his emphasis from vodka to his Ole George rye whiskey and bourbon. The consumer preference for brown spirits caught him off-guard. "I didn't start our aged-whiskey program fast enough," he says. "The three-year barrel aging set us back. Now barrels are in short supply."

This year, Rabish expects profits to soar. Michigan passed a law allowing the state's growing collection of craft distillers to sell directly to customers through tasting rooms. "Our new goal is to sell 75 percent of our product direct to consumers. There are no lost margins to distributors and retailers on the revenue coming in the tasting room door. No transportation costs or delays on receivables. We get to meet our consumers and tell our story." To celebrate, Grand Traverse customers will have the opportunity to create their own whiskey—choosing a corn, rye, wheat, malted barley, or peated malted barley distillate to age in small charred oak casks at home.

Insights from craft producers such as Rabish offer benchmarks for progress you can expect your own craft distillery to meet. These are cautionary tales as well. You will want to

tip

Do you have the patience for distilling? Think before you answer. Rabish didn't appreciate how much quicker and easier whiskey was to produce. "With vodka, I have to distill, distill, distill" to get to 190 proof. But whiskey isn't a neutral spirit. It is a one-time shot through a three-plate still, a much faster and easier process. Costs for holding the spirits in barrels are higher, but the overall profit margins are fatter. Named after his grandfather, Ole George now accounts for 65 percent of Rabish's sales; he has 200 barrels aging at the distillery and has moved to a 24-hour, seven-day-a-week production schedule.

avoid miscalculating the relative cost of producing whiskey and vodka. And if you want to make whiskey, you will start that project Day One. Every bit of advice producers offer cost them precious time and resources. To be true to the craft code, they share their stories to help the next wave of craft producers.

Albemarle CiderWorks, Rural Ridge Farm, North Garden, Virginia
Bud, Charlotte, Chuck, Anne, and Bill Shelton, Operators
Founded 2009

The siblings bought Rural Ridge Farm for their parents 30 years ago, a small farm close to Charlottesville where their father, Bud Shelton, could retire as a gentleman farmer. A then-nascent movement to rescue disappearing heirloom apple varieties by planting orchards had started in the area and the family signed on. Today, the siblings are partners in a thriving nursery and orchard, with a cidery the natural last step in the evolution of their apple adventure. After all, hard cider is why apples were grown in Virginia in the first place.

The Sheltons planted hundreds of varieties of apple trees in their original orchard, says Charlotte Shelton, the business brains of the family. "There is such a dramatic nuance of flavor in appledom. It was going to be lost with the heirlooms falling by the wayside. We are interested in preserving this culinary and cultural heritage. A historian by training, this resonated particularly with me and the boys." One brother runs the nursery and orchard and another is the cider maker.

The family forged ahead slowly. Virginia Vintage Apples became a commercial nursery in 2000, and Albemarle CiderWorks (www.albemarleciderworks.com) launched in 2009. "We are reasonably intelligent. Most of it is common sense. We cross-examine ourselves and have different skill sets, and are good at different things. And we're proud of that. You can't let ego get involved. It doesn't matter who does what," says Shelton.

Even though they had the land and the apples, building the cidery required construction of a cider house and tasting room large enough to host events—roughly $1 million in personal savings and a loan against the farm. "We were in a state of complete shock by the time we figured it all out. But by then we were committed to it and we waded right on in," says Shelton.

Apples cost $12 to $20 a bushel, and each bushel yields one case of finished hard cider. The first year the Sheltons produced 900 cases and now produce three times that amount. "We're feeling our way along" to see how much cider to produce, she says. Royal Pippin was their first single varietal cider introduced in 2009. Old Virginia Winesap was introduced in 2010. They now have eight cider varieties for sale. The cidery was cash-flow positive its third year and may soon turn a profit.

The Sheltons bought their farm and planted their orchards before even thinking about making hard cider, so they had a head start in the hard cider business. Still, they were surprised by the cost of the cider making equipment. A list of the major pieces of equipment and what they cost is a reminder to grow slowly. You only want to invest in the equipment you absolutely need.

Big-ticket items:

▶ Apple press—$30,000
▶ Chiller—$22,000
▶ Six German double-jacketed stainless steel tanks—$40,000
▶ Pressure-filler bottler—$10,000
▶ Multiple pumps—$5,000 each

Cider making is not cheap. As you can see from this list, the process involves more than pressing apples. Gather plenty of financial and anecdotal information about the upfront costs of cider making before you write that first big check. If you're in it to win it, be prepared to lay out significant funds at the outset.

The cidery remains a mission for the Sheltons. "We're interested in restoring cider to its rightful place in libations. We enjoy the notion that we are preserving rare apple varieties," says Shelton. "The cider industry is very, very young. We're just in the first years of it. What is it going to be in 50 years? If we don't let it get run off the road by the beer companies that are just looking to increase their market share by making a cider novelty, I think it is possible that well-crafted hard ciders will stand alone as a category. That future is tied to a revival of heirloom apples."

> **tip**
>
> Grassroots marketing is the way to go in this particular business. Reach out and get to know your buyers, says Charlotte Shelton. "We have to proselytize. We sell to the wine market, not the beer market," she says, noting that the cider-tasting room has been their smartest business investment. Self-distributors, their workshops and festivals at the farm are essential to spreading the word about hard cider. They want the business to remain in the family forever.

Alchemy & Science, Burlington, Vermont
Boston Beer Company, Owner
Founded 2011

When Alan Newman sold his Pennsylvania craft brewery, Magic Hat Brewing Company, Jim Koch invited him to create a new division within Boston Beer that incubates microbreweries. He would be ripping a page from the MillerCoors playbook for its Tenth &

Block craft division, only Newman and Boston Beer had craft cred. "My mission is to grow craft's market share in ways Boston Beer would never think of," Newman says. In three years, he has launched a new national beer brand and two microbreweries, with a third under construction.

Newman created Traveler Beer Company to be the holding company for Shandies, a wheat ale infused with fresh citrus juice, an American version of the British tradition of mixing citrus soda with beer for a light quaffer. Shandies initial sales are promising enough, he says, to justify a national rollout this year. A second attempt at launching a national brand—Just Beer's Anytime IPA, a lower alcohol light beer—crashed on takeoff. "Everyone is making session [lower alcohol] beers now. You can't make one separate from a brewery."

Microbreweries are expensive gambles, and Newman is launching them in far-flung corners of the country. "These are opportunistic breweries," he says, explaining that the three cities he chose are in underserved markets. Angel City Brewery was a defunct Los Angeles brand he picked up in January 2012, along with its 10,000-square-foot warehouse space in the emerging downtown Los Angeles arts district. He built a small, on-site brewery, relying on food trucks to provide taproom grub for the young crowd frequenting this emerging section of the city. Using Boston Beer's breweries and distributors, Angel City beers are available throughout Southern California.

Newman employs a similar concept at his Miami-based Concrete Beach Brewery located in the Wynwood arts district, this time with Latin-themed beers. The start-from-scratch operation, launched a year after Angel City, was slow to open, in large part due to the notoriously craft-averse Florida regulatory process. Although it was his third project, purchased in August 2013 from founder Jeremy Cowen of Shmaltz Brewing Company [note: Shmaltz Brewing Co. no longer exists] Coney Island Brewing is up and brewing on the famous boardwalk. Buying an existing brewery with ongoing operations is the easiest way to jump into a market. The only challenge is marketing the beer, which is Newman's forte.

The economies of starting a company within a larger brewer are substantial, says Newman. Boston Beer takes care of backroom functions such as human resources, accounting and legal, and gives Alchemy & Science (www.alchemyandscience.com) access to its network of giant regional breweries to produce the beer it sells in grocery stores using Boston Beer's powerful distribution

aha!

Start small to win big. "The opportunity is building neighborhood breweries," says Alan Newman. "We focus on being part of the local community with each of our brands."

network. Newman has his own sales teams and supply systems, but he has access to the parent company's lower bulk prices and can piggyback on Boston Beer whenever it makes sense.

Newman spends his time traveling between his still-struggling, small businesses and doesn't have an office in the parent company's Boston headquarters. And he never will. "Jim thought we would end up doing things the Boston Beer way, which was the opposite of what he wants," says Newman. "Jim allows us to not have a plan, to bring him the opportunities we see."

Craft beer is a capital-intensive business, says Newman. His job is to figure out how to make it less so. "With so many new breweries, there is too much beer, too many brands, too few open taps at bars, too little space on retail beer shelves. Something is going to happen to clear things out. It's just not clear what is going to start the chain reaction. It may be as simple as the Millennials settling down to their favorite brands and no longer trying every beer they see."

What's next for A&S? So far, Koch has approved every concept Newman's brought him, he says. Now he has to make those concepts, and Koch's trust in him, pay off.

Greenbar Craft Distillery, Los Angeles, California
Melkon Khosrovian and Litty Mathew, Owners
Founded 2004

Greenbar Craft Distillery (www.greenbar.biz) is a partnership between former software engineer Melkon Khosrovian and his Cordon Bleu-trained wife, Litty Mathew. Khosrovian sold a software company he started to turn their hobby infusing neutral spirits with locally sourced fruits and botanicals into a commercial operation. "We had no business plan," he says. "Our friends liked our infusions, so we thought there was a market for what we made."

To allow them to focus solely on infusions, Khosrovian created a cooperative scheme with independent producers sharing marketing and distribution. "We only wanted to make vodkas and gins. We brought in partners who wanted to make other spirits," he says. The idea was that a larger portfolio of products would be easier to sell. It soon became clear, however, "the only thing anyone wanted to share was the rewards," he says. "The economy tanked in 2008. The investors disappeared. It was a monumental failure." With hundreds of thousands of dollars of their own money invested in the venture, the couple doubled down to produce the larger portfolio of products themselves.

Now independent, they committed wholeheartedly to a hyper-local, strictly organic approach to off-the-wall flavored spirits. The goal made them a darling of local politicians and, with a $250,000 loan from the Los Angeles Community Redevelopment Agency, they bought their current downtown location in 2012 and became a grain-to-glass distillery. Committed to full disclosure about every aspect of their operation, Khosrovian and his wife opened a tasting room overlooking the distillery two years later.

For white spirits, they use a wheat wash, which the couple believes "lifts" flavors and aromas of infusions like their Tru celery/dill/fennel vodka. Their Slow Hand Six Woods Malt Organic Whiskey is 100 percent malted barley and aged in an oversize charred oak barrel with hickory, grape, mulberry, red oak, and hard maple blocks thrown in for added flavor. They make bitters, liqueurs, rum, and tequila, which they produce in a rented distillery in Mexico. Everything is packaged in eco-friendly lightweight bottles with 100 percent recycled labels. They plant a tree for every bottle sold (400,000 trees and counting).

The idea of joining forces with other spirits producers didn't die. Greenbar's success is due in large part to contract distilling. "We design products for our clients and produce them in our distillery," says Khosrovian, noting they have both pot stills and continuous column stills. Without that, the arcane liquor laws would have killed them, he says. "We didn't see how hard it would be. We had to sign contracts with distributors—Mafia-like deals—that locked us in for life. It was a total surprise. We couldn't believe it was legal to demand these kinds of payments. I can't ask [our distributor] to do anything without paying them money to incentivize them to do their job. You can't leave a bad relationship in this industry. The little guys—we are fledglings in a world created for elephants," says Khosrovian.

California does not allow spirits producers to sell their products at the distillery or to self-distribute, as craft brewers can. "Ninety percent of the successful craft distillers in the country make it on sales from their distillery. Tasting rooms are the cash cow. In California, wholesalers fought us tooth and nail before the craft distillers won the right to have tasting rooms where people could at least sample our products. But we are limited to quarter-ounce tastes."

Besides the ongoing battle to loosen state sales and distribution laws, Khosrovian says his biggest challenge is maintaining the consistency clients such as Darden Restaurant Group and Whole Foods Market demand. "We have had to become control freaks," he says.

Craft Brew Alliance (CBA), Portland, Oregon
Public Company One-Third Owned by Anheuser-Busch
Brands include: Redhook, Widmer Brothers, Kona, Omission, Square Mile Cider
Founded 2008

"Margins for very small craft brewers are good now; really, really good," Andy Thomas, Craft Brew Alliance's (http://craftbrew.com) CEO, told the craft brewers attending a recent

Brewbound business conference. But each rung up the craft beer ladder—bottling beer instead of just delivering kegs, salesmen to get those bottles into stores, expanding capacity to meet increased sales, multistate distribution, and mass marketing to support increased production—adds costs that will squeeze those margins. It is a long, difficult, slow climb to become a brewery big enough to have the market efficiencies necessary to regain those lost profit margins.

CBA is feeling that squeeze. Its profit margins fell during the past several years, even as revenues rose and sales climbed to give it 4.3 percent of the craft beer market. The increased competition from the rush of new small breweries into the market only makes the fight for profitability more difficult.

Banding together with other brewers to grow more quickly is the CBA model. The alliance was formed around an initial public offering of stock out of necessity in 2008 at the end of craft beer's devastating no-growth decade. Anheuser-Busch partnered with two icons of craft brewing, Portland-based Widmer, launched in 1984 by Kurt and Rob Widmer, and Seattle-based Redhook. Hawaii's Kona Brewing sold to CBA in 2010. The company launched the gluten-free Omission brand of beer in 2012 and Square Mile Cider Company in 2013. Anheuser-Busch owns 32 percent of CBA.

Appalachian Mountain Brewery (http://appalachianmountainbrewery.com) signed a strategic sales and distribution partnership with CBA in December 2014. Also a public company, the small North Carolina brewery's razor-thin margins have depressed its stock price, even though its third-quarter revenue was $266,283, up 38 percent compared to the previous quarter and up 77 percent compared to the same quarter in 2013, due in part to the introduction of a new line of craft hard cider.

Through CBA, Appalachian will have access to Anheuser-Busch's powerful national distribution and sales apparatus, one of the drivers of CBA's 24 percent increase in adjusted operating income in its 2014 fiscal year and 11 percent growth in sales. For its part, CBA gets "the opportunity to be 'local' while expanding our reach into North Carolina," says Thomas.

Back in 2010 when Widmer and Redhook jumped into bed with Anheuser-Busch, the rest of the craft beer industry was shocked. The Brewers Association kicked CBA out of the craft club, a move that still stings. "We consider ourselves to be craft, regardless of the Brewers Association definition," says Kurt Widmer, a CBA director and former board member of the craft beer association, who has no regrets. Anheuser-Busch "has been very good to work with," he says. "They are committed to quality. Joining with them allowed us to have state-of-the art facilities. They've lived up to their commitment to us even though we're both independent public companies in competition with each other.

CBA operates as one company with the various brands sharing marketing, breweries, and distribution. Anheuser-Busch allows them to use its purchasing power to lower the cost of supplies, he adds. When there was an equipment failure at a brewery and the vendor estimated three to five weeks before the brewery would be back online, Anheuser-Busch stepped in and it was fixed in 24 hours.

It's an advantage that other breweries are interested in sharing, he says. "We get calls all of the time from breweries who want to join our club. We're in conversations with several breweries now. It makes sense for us to be bigger, more efficient. It is possible that a shakeout is coming. I'm not going to say we're guaranteed success, but we have all we need to succeed."

fun fact

Some analysts are bullish and predict Craft Brew Alliance sales will grow by more than 300 percent during the next three years, with profits expected to grow from $3.1 million in 2014 to $8.3 million on revenues exceeding $220 million in 2016.

Despite increases in operating income and sales, CBA's stock price was down 10 percent for the year in December 2014 with the company reporting slowing sales growth attributable to the increasingly crowded craft beer market. Over the five years it has been publicly traded, CBA stock has increased more than 300 percent in value and is now considered overpriced based on current earnings and the company's difficulty sustaining profit margins while it invests to grow sales.

Just as in the last shakeout that started in the late 1990s, "the breweries who won't make it are the ones who stop making beer their main thing and screw up the quality," says Widmer. "Breweries that are not adequately financed often sell beer that should be sewered" or thrown down the drain.

Troy Cider, Sebastopol, California
Mark McTavish, Owner
Founded 2012

Old, overgrown apple orchards were everywhere Troy Carter looked when he took a post-college motorcycle trek along the back roads of California's Sonoma Coast. Planted in the 1950s, the trees had been fending for themselves in the generations since wine arrived. A kombucha fan, Carter treasured artisan hard cider's funky flavors and guessed the ugly apples were the perfect raw material for his favorite libation.

The first pressing of Troy Cider was in the fall of 2012 using the mostly Gravenstein apples he and about 100 of his Stanford University friends harvested one afternoon. To manage the wild yeast fermentation, Carter hired organic winemaker Tony Coturri to produce his inaugural vintage. Artisan hard cider makers view cider apples and orchards much like vintners view wine grapes and vineyards. The taste of the "place" is in the cider.

Fresh-pressed juice with nothing but the orchard's natural wild yeast, cold fermented in pinot noir barrels, Carter's cider made itself. He aged it for eight months before bottling it, unfiltered. The next year Carter made Troy at Sonoma's Old World Winery with winemaker Derek Trowbridge overseeing fermentation.

The 25-year-old, who thought to check out the apples by the side of the road, moved on in his journey around the world. While Carter remains the "artist in residence," he sold his cider operation to Mark McTavish, whose 2-year-old company Half Pint Ciders imports and distributes hard cider in Los Angeles. McTavish says he will stick to Carter's protocol. The third vintage of Troy was released at the end of 2014.

Still using the wild fruit, the third vintage grew to 50 barrels to meet rising demand for the funky, dry, low-alcohol drink. With 20,000, 500 ml bottles priced at $10, the business is thriving. McTavish added a traditional quince, pear, and apple blend to the Troy portfolio. The rest of the hard ciders McTavish sells are from Spain, Canada, and other parts of the U.S. Northwest. "It's an easy sell. Once people taste it, they want it. But they don't know where to find it. I'm the first cider-only distributor in the Los Angeles market," he says.

Eager to capture hard cider's sudden popularity, McTavish is planning to launch another cider brand, 101 Cider House, and open a cidery and taproom in Westlake Village in Los Angeles' San Fernando Valley in 2015. The juice is pressed to order and shipped to the Westlake Village from Oregon, where he ferments and ages it in 100 used tequila barrels. "All wild yeast. Nothing pasteurized. No sulfur. Just raw juice," says McTavish.

Harlem Brewing, Harlem, New York
Celeste Beatty, Owner
Founded 2001

Celeste Beatty made a long-term bet on herself when she launched Harlem Brewing (www.harlembrewing.com) in 2001, selling her home and liquidating her 401(k) to pull together the $500,000 to launch a beer brand based on recipes she created homebrewing in her Harlem kitchen. The new Harlem Renaissance was underway, and she believed that her neighbors would embrace a craft beer made for them. She named her signature beer after a Harlem neighborhood called Sugar Hill, from the lyrics of Duke Ellington's song "Take the A Train."

"I compare my homebrew process to a jam session," says Beatty. "You have improvisation and transformation of notes and ingredients to make a unique brew. Most times I am listening to Sarah Vaughn when I am homebrewing." Beatty pays homage to the culinary heritage of beer making among African women by infusing cumin, coriander, and grains of paradise, a West African spice, into her beers.

"I focus on making a good product and being connected to everything that goes into every step of production. The nature of craft beer is to stay small and special. It is all about quality and keeping it real," she says.

Beatty contracted with Olde Saratoga Brewing Company (www.harlembrewing.com) in upstate New York to produce her Sugar Hill Golden Ale and other beers, initially distributing them herself in an old SUV that accommodated 25 cases of beer. With her son managing marketing and sales, she says, "It is one beer at a time, one restaurant at a time," making a direct, personal connection with customers. She estimates she pours her beers at 200 events a year, which is her primary marketing effort.

The quality of her beer and her dogged determination caught the attention of former President Bill Clinton, who invited Beatty to participate in the 2006 Clinton Foundation Entrepreneur's program. Through the program, she was partnered with craft beer veteran Pete Slosberg, founder of Pete's Wicked Ale, who continues to help Beatty establish her brand.

While her beers are served in legendary Harlem restaurants, including Sylvia's, Red Rooster, The Cecil, Minton's and Chez Lucienne, after 14 years of many ups and downs, real growth has been gradual. Beatty currently produces 3,000 barrels of beer a year. That will change in 2015, she says. She plans to build a brewery at an old family farm in Saratoga Springs, where she has already started growing her own hops. This year, she also plans to open a Harlem Brewery taproom in its namesake neighborhood and ramp up exports to Japan, Sweden, and England.

"I am always working, but it is my love and joy. I love that this business is about hospitality and being green—gardening, farming, cooking, community empowerment, building local economies, as well as bringing people together," she says, noting that a favorite gift to her clients are garlands of hops from her farm, which look like Hawaiian leis.

What is the worst thing about the beer business? Kegs! "Having kegs is like having 30 children. You have to keep track of each keg to bring it back home. It's expensive

tip

Get investors on board early. The earlier, the better, in fact. "My big mistake? Not partnering with investors sooner than now," she says, noting that financing growth is an ongoing struggle. "Not listening to good advice was a mistake. I had opportunities to form partnerships. But I did not see a good fit. It is a great struggle to keep my business going. If you don't have investors, you will be bootstrapping so much that it can become overwhelming. So don't wait too long to have a plan to get capital."

and time-consuming. Kegs get lost. Restaurants are supposed to return them, but they put empty kegs out the back door and they often are stolen," says Beatty.

Wormtown Brewery, Worcester, Massachusetts
Ben Roesch, Tom Oliveri and David Fields, Owners
Founded 2009

"A piece of Mass in every glass" is Wormtown Brewery's declaration (http://worm townbrewery.com). Even though they were the first brewery in Massachusetts' second largest city, by 2009, Wormtown was late to New England's craft beer party. To set their beers apart, Massachusetts-grown and -produced ingredients would be the goal. For the Mass Whole line of beers, all the ingredients would come from local growers—the hops down to the grain malted at Valley Malt, the first malt house to open in New England in 100 years. Wormtown joined Valley Malt's "Brewer Supported Agriculture" initiative, with long-term malt contracts.

"We've had success with Mass Whole," says Ben Roesch, Wormtown's brewer. "Whether that's because we've priced it the same as conventional beers or because of the local ingredients or that it's just a good beer, I'm not sure. I don't know if our customers care about local ingredients. But it is important to me as the person making the purchasing decisions." That is a big commitment for a new brewery. Roesch believes fresh malt adds a layer of flavor beyond what is possible with industrially malted grain. But his insistence on local ingredients is also a philosophical position: small businesses should support other small businesses.

The original Wormtown brewery that opened in 2010 was certainly small, designed to make enough beer to supply the two restaurants owned by Roesch's partner, Tom Oliveri. The ten-barrel brewhouse fit nicely into a 1,000-square-foot storefront next to one of his cafes. "Being Worcester's local beer was the vision," says Oliveri.

They hit a soft target. Wormtown sales doubled from 1,000 barrels ($200,000) in 2010 to 2,500 barrels

warning

You're a brewer, distiller, or cider maker. You are not, however, a distributor. That's a whole other industry. So, leave the distributing to the experts. "We started self-distributing to get the full sales [dollars], as opposed to using a distributor who takes a portion of sales," says Ben Roesch. "If you are self-distributing, you drop off a keg on the first of the month, and the bar has until the end of the next month to pay you. You have a receivable on your books for 60 days." And you are in the collection business, which is a pain. "We quickly gave that up."

($400,000) in 2012 and were 3,000 barrels ($800,000) by 2014 with profit margins between 15 percent and 17 percent. The new brewery opening in early 2015 allows them to produce up to 30,000 barrels a year. "One of the smartest things we did was to spend money on radio advertising to kick off our canning of Be Hoppy IPA. Demand for our flagship beer just exploded," says Oliveri.

It helped that after their first five years they added a third partner, David Fields, a former Anheuser-Busch distributor. In an unusual twist, joining the business coincided with Fields selling his family's beer distributorship. While Oliveri financed the first brewery with a $250,000 bank loan, Fields covered the $3 million cost of building the second one. "As we stand today, we are a debt-free company, aside from the money that's owed to David [Fields]. If we believe in something and spending money is going to make us more money or help us, I have no problem doing it. When you have that freedom, it's a lot easier for any business."

And what they want to do is double down on local. "We are taking the Mass Whole series and bringing in Massachusetts herbs and spices and vegetables beyond pumpkin," says Roesch. "Our Warthog Wheat is named after the variety of wheat that the owners of Valley Malt grow. We'll use it on the label and tell the story of Valley Malt."

"As the entire globe has become more intrigued by local ingredients and local everything, it gives us credibility," says Fields. "We are committed to local, both at the senior management level and our field staff. Our sales reps have a story to tell. It matters, no question about it. Because our new brewery has twice the capacity, I thought we would add some geography to our distribution. But as I met with distributors, I realized our brand had a lot more room to grow within our existing footprint. Our brand can grow deeper in Worcester."

Green Star Brewing, Chicago, Illinois
Michael and Helen Cameron, Owners
Founded 2014

When is a brewery attached to a restaurant not a brewpub? When it sits next to one of Michael and Helen Cameron's Uncommon Ground (www.uncommonground.com) restaurants in Chicago. Celebrated for their extraordinary environmental activism, the couple serves seriously good farm-to-table fare using organic ingredients. And from the moment they opened their first eatery in 1991, they wanted to have house-made beers on their menu. The perfect location—next door to their original restaurant—became available in 2012.

They built a modest seven-barrel brewhouse designed to serve only in-house needs and funded the $250,000 project through personal savings and a small bank loan. The

---

▶ Read It . . .

Read these books to find more stories from the front lines of the craft revolution:

The Art of Distilling Whiskey and Other Stories, Bill Owens and Alan Dikty, (Quarry Books, 2009)

The Audacity of Hops: The History of America's Craft Beer Revolution, Tom Acitelli, (Chicago Review Press, 2013)

Bourbon Strange: Surprising Stories of American Whiskey, Charles K. Cowdery, (Made and Bottled in Kentucky, 2014)

---

space needed structural reinforcement and a search for inexpensive used equipment was fruitless, so the project was more expensive than they expected, but only modestly so. The couple pays a premium for organic ingredients—going so far as having a supplier grow their yeast on organic grain—but the cost is in line with the organic products they buy for their restaurant.

"We have always educated our staff and our customers, continually talking about the seasonality of our products, always using the best and the ripest produce. And now we can talk about the best seasonal beers to match our seasonal food," says Cameron. "We are very consciously making a closed-loop brewery. Some of our spent grains go into our vegan spent grain and black quinoa burger, and some are dried and ground into flour we used in our Parmesan bread sticks. The rest goes to a local chicken farmer for feed."

Their tagline is "do-good beer." Green Star Brewing is the first certified organic brewery in Illinois. Beyond going to local beer festivals, they do little to actively market their beer.

tip

Yes, the craft business is on a quick upswing, and you have to be ready to pounce on the opportunities. But patience does come in handy, especially when you are waiting to see if your gamble pays off. "You can accomplish anything with time and money," says Michael Cameron. "It just took us more time, 23 years, to get the money."

6

The Craft Customer

n October 2014, the Brewers Association held their 32nd Annual Great American Beer Festival, the longest-running gathering of craft brewers and craft beer drinkers in the country and by far the largest with nearly 50,000 people attending the Denver event. The T-shirt-and-jeans crowd was searching for what's new, what's different, what's next in craft beer: sour beers, bourbon barrel-aged beers, and wacky brews from off-the-grid nooks and crannies in the country that are just getting their first neighborhood breweries. With 700 breweries showcasing 3,000 beers, it was impossible for anyone to see it all.

That's why beer fans love the craft revolution. Corporate giants may pad their wallets peddling a stream of cheap "refreshment," but these crazy craft artisans stand behind their tasty stouts and hoppy IPAs with pride. Their mantra: the bottom line takes care of itself if you make good beer. The best of the craft distillers and artisan hard cider makers follow the same business logic. In this black-and-white world, craft's success is a thumb in the eye of corporate America, Wall Street, and Madison Avenue all at once.

The craft consumer has been a reflection of this culture and, logically, craft producers approached their customers as so many Mini-Mes. They designed their promotions to appeal first and foremost to themselves.

> **aha!**
>
> Harness the love of the craft fanbase—all of them. "Craft beer drinkers used to be 30- to 45-year-old guys. Now everyone is drinking craft right out of the gate; it's everyone's first beer. Brewers are like chefs, they have fans now," says Michelle Soltys, co-owner of Pacific Stainless Systems, a San Diego-based brewhouse manufacturer.

Generation Craft

Going forward, the mass audience will be driving sales, if the sector is to continue its rapid growth. It presents a new set of challenges, although at this point craft's fastest-growing audience is the masses of Millennials. Highly individualized and independent, America's young adults have both the group-conscience to want to change the world for the better and the self-assuredness to believe they know how to do it.

The current surge in demand for craft directly tracks the rising number of Millennials (people born between the early 1980s and early 2000s) reaching legal drinking age. The generation's peak birth year turned 25 years old in 2014. Craft reflects their particular preference for local, environmentally sustainable products, and while these beverages may cost a little more, they are affordable luxuries that reflect this generation's idea of sophistication and education. Enough of this generation is happy to pay a bit more to drink something they believe is special to shift the whole market upscale. If that preference becomes a habit, craft will become the main event in alcoholic beverages.

The Rise of Big Craft

The question is how will customers behave in a future where "craft" is less clearly defined? The most successful craft brewers are now major national companies. Big Beer is launching craft-ish brands as well as buying up small craft breweries to cash in on the craft craze. Some craft distillers are masquerading industrially made spirits as "handmade." The leading producers in the burgeoning hard cider sector are pumping out this new libation on a massive industrial scale. According to consumer research from Craft Brew Alliance, more beer shoppers identify Blue Moon, produced by MillerCoors, as "craft" than correctly identify either Sierra Nevada or Lagunitas as craft beer brands.

At the current inflection point, craft consumers are still identifiable. They crave novelty and will pay a premium to be surprised and delighted with what is in their glass. When it comes to beer, the failure of traditional brands to inspire is fairly universal. With spirits, it is less about being offended by what has been on offer from large producers and more of an eagerness to discover something new. Hard cider customers are discovering a whole new category, which female drinkers are particularly pleased is lower-calorie than beer or wine and gluten-free.

> **tip**
>
> Generate buzz through good word of mouth via social media. Unlike America's wine culture, craft customers are not collecting or otherwise following what widely recognized authorities define as the "best." They trust their friends to tell them what's good and rely on social media to communicate that knowledge.

Craft consumers know when they find what they are looking for and have favorites, but that doesn't stop them from continuing to explore new craft offerings. While there is an aspect of seeking the rare and elusive, craft consumers have enough of the pub crawler in them to offset the snobbishness of drinking a "better" beer.

Big Beer distributors see things differently. There are solid reasons to believe the current craft audience is an aberration, says Lester Jones, chief economist for the National Beer Wholesalers Association (www.nbwa.org). The Bud drinker hasn't died; he's just been dormant. The craft boom tracks the rising fortunes of the top 1 percent of all American consumers as much as it tracks Millennials. "Right now, there is a high-end gold rush chasing them." The question is whether the four million people today aged 21 to 34 will continue to pay a premium for alcoholic beverages as they age. "Not everyone is going to drink Dom Perignon. Eventually, most consumers step down to inexpensive cavas."

Of greater concern for craft producers, says Greg Koch, cofounder of Stone Brewing Company in San Diego, is a consumer who unknowingly trades down when they buy "craft-ish" products, such as Anheuser-Busch's Shock Top. "Most Americans aren't paying attention. The downside of fooling customers is very low and the upside is high," says Koch. Craft producers can claim the moral high ground, but will consumers continue to care?

When the craft movement began in the late 1980s, the interest in drinking a better beer drove the craft beer market, which went from zero to capture 5 percent of the total American beer market. Subsequent generations joined the movement, but it plateaued during the decade from the late 1990s until the late 2000s. When the first of the Boomer offspring reached legal drinking age, the market took off again. The Brewers Association predicts craft beer will account for 20 percent of the overall American beer market by 2020.

According to Brewers Association statistics, in 2001, the median craft beer drinker was a 39-year-old, highly educated, white male with a relatively high income living in a region served by several local craft breweries. Today, 75 percent of adults of legal drinking age live within ten miles of a brewery. The Millennial drinker brings a broader spectrum of Americans to the craft party, with women now constituting 15 percent of the craft beer market.

Overall, beer continues to lose market share to other alcoholic beverages: beer was 55 percent of the market in 2000, dropping to 49 percent in 2011, while spirits' market share rose from 29 percent to 34 percent in the same period, according to Demeter Group Investment Bank. Yet craft beer's strength in the beer market is growing rapidly. "Despite crafts' thinly resourced marketing and sales departments, five of the fastest-growing beer brands are craft—Dale's Pale Ale from Oskar Blues Brewery, Lagunitas' India Pale Ale, Ranger IPA from New Belgium, Torpedo Extra IPA from Sierra Nevada, and Shiner Light from Gambrinus.

The Craft Identity

Craft drinkers are experimenters; nonlinear explorers who jump from one new beer or spirits or hard cider to another without an obvious, discernable progression, says Demeter. Their omnivorous tendency tracks styles rather than brands. They are pushing the overall market toward a style-first identity—they overwhelmingly favor hoppy IPA beers—and away from the brand-first identity that has long dominated beer consumption. The extremists among them drive the development of new

tip

Embrace the "day drinking" market. These younger drinkers are driving a new and somewhat unexpected demand for lower alcohol, lighter bodied craft beers that can be drunk all day, often referred to as session beers. "We will be introducing a year-round pilsner in 2015 called 'Nooner Pilsner,' says Sierra Nevada's Ken Grossman, noting that he has produced plenty of lighter lagers over the years, but this current effort is driven by consumer demand. Supermarket sales of Session IPAs grew 339 percent in 2014, according to IRI.

breweries with their willingness to try every new beer they find.

The craft drinker wants to feel a connection to what is in their glass, says Christian McMahan, a principal in Smartfish, a Connecticut-based marketing firm specializing in craft beverages. Speaking to Brewbound in December, he told new brewers to tell their personal stories to consumers. "Authenticity matters" to Millennial drinkers, McMahan says. They will drop a product that makes them feel manipulated by false hype.

The craft drinker knows more about what they drink than noncraft drinkers, according to surveys by market research firm IBISWorld. They are health-conscious consumers choosing higher-quality beverages. And they tend to do most of their drinking at home.

The overall improvement of the economy expected to continue for the next five years will buoy the craft sectors, according to IBISWorld. "Improving disposable incomes will enable more consumers to fit high-end products like craft beer into their budgets. Changing consumer preferences, driven in part by the buy-local movement and a political push against large corporations that stemmed from the financial meltdown, drove up demand for small breweries. Per-capita consumption of beer is higher among 21- to 35-year-olds than other age groups. The proportion of the overall population within this age range, and its increasing disposable income, will have a positive effect on demand for beer during the next five years." This age group is expected to account for more than 32 percent of craft beer sales in 2015, according to IBISWorld analysts.

The craft shopper knows what they like, says David Hayslette, a marketing strategist with MeadWestVaco packaging suppliers, whose research shows that 73 percent of craft consumers say they usually know what beer they are looking for when they enter a store. Yet they are extremely open to discovery, he says, noting that 64 percent say they buy something new after reading the craft packaging. On average, craft shoppers spend four and a half minutes reading beer labels. This compares with 30 seconds spent by the average Anheuser-Busch or MillerCoors customer.

Thomas Touring, director of restaurant operations for the House of Blues chain of music venues, says he shifted his restaurants to an all-craft beer menu because his customers were

warning

To you, your brew is the best thing going. But to others, it may be a bit "meh." Accept that you won't be all things to all people. "Craft beer isn't for everyone," says Dennis Hartman, manager of the craft beer department with Wine Warehouse (www.winewarehouse. com), a leading California distributor. That sense of being something "special" is why people drink it. No one wants to feel ordinary anymore.

demanding local beers. Once he made the shift, beer sales went up and so did food sales. "The bottom line is that a lot more people were coming in to House of Blues."

International Markets

Consumers outside of the United States are responding to craft alcoholic beverages too. Demand for American craft alcoholic beverages is rising around the world, says Dennis Hartman with distributor Wine Warehouse. Ten years ago, American breweries couldn't sell beer to the Mexican market; now, the Mexicans are clamoring for U.S. craft beers. Vietnam, Philippines, and Thailand are small countries with improving economies and a thirst for American craft beer. In five years, they likely will be making their own craft beers, but for now they are importing as much as they can get. With the big beer companies focused on China and Russia, craft is dominating these smaller markets.

American craft beer exports reached $100 million in 2014, according to the Brewers Association. Sales rose 64 percent in Brazil and 38 percent in the Asia-Pacific region. There are now 80 craft brewers exporting beer to international markets by the end of 2014.

Craftport (www.craftport.com), a small Portland, Oregon-based craft beer and spirits exporter focused on Latin American and Southeast Asian markets, is just getting started in this game. "The growing middle class in developing countries wants American craft products. They are educated and they've traveled abroad and want to have at home what they experienced when they were in America," says Lars Burkholder, Craftport's regional account executive for Latin America and Brazil.

Michael Vachon, founder of Maverick Drinks (http://maverickdrinks.com), an American craft spirits importer in England, says young Brits are wild for "hands-on" spirits. The word "craft" is important, he says, because consumers understand it means something special. "It was very easy to move up to craft beer, and craft beer set the scene for craft spirits. Consumers have come to appreciate its authenticity. It means it is a better product." The very American-ness of craft adds to the allure, Vachon says. "Bourbon and rye are on the rise. The U.K. is so dominated by the big brands that people find small brands exciting."

Exports of American craft beer are expected to rise at an annualized rate of 16.3 percent between 2015 and 2020, according to IBISWorld analysts. "Exports are forecast to be a major source of industry growth during the next five years because neighboring markets are relatively untapped by craft breweries. A weak U.S. dollar, especially compared to the Canadian dollar, is expected to benefit craft brewers as they expand distribution contracts with the northern neighbor. Exports of American craft beer are expected to rise at an annualized rate of 16.3 percent between 2015 and 2020," according to IBISWorld analysts.

Because of varying state-by-state regulations, "it is easier now to sell beer internationally than to a different state," says Keith Lemcke, vice president of Chicago-based Siebel Institute of Technology and marketing manager for the World Brewing Academy. International demand is growing so fast you can feel it rise in places like the Nordic countries, Argentina, Brazil, and Columbia.

At the same time, according to IBISWorld, American craft consumers' thirst for variety extends to the emerging foreign craft beer industry, driving growth in this category during the next five years, especially as disposable income expands. As a result, craft beer imports are projected to grow at an average annual rate of 6.8 percent through 2020.

In the meantime, the Great American Beer Festival in October 2015 is on track to be even bigger, and the Brewers Association will be featuring many more non-U.S. craft beers.

Everywhere there are young drinkers, the audience for craft beverages is growing. Never assume that because a city or state hasn't responded to craft before that they aren't interested. The quality of that region's early craft producers may have been inconsistent. Or perhaps the legislature was particularly slow in providing the necessary regulatory relief to foster craft producers. The common denominator of underserved niches is a simple lack of exposure to good craft beverages.

If you see an underserved niche, jump on it. Chances are, folks in that corner of the world don't know what they are missing. When you expose them to craft products, they will respond. At the same time, no market in the U.S. can be described as "saturated" regardless of how crowded it appears. New craft producers in San Diego; Portland, Oregon; New York City; and Chicago are struggling to keep up with demand. Craft sales are increasing everywhere.

Financing Craft Beverage Companies

Tap the shoulder of anyone involved in the craft alcoholic beverage world and ask where to find money to launch a new brewery, distillery, or cidery, and they will immediately respond, "Anywhere and everywhere." Craft businesses may be hard work, but finding the money to open them has become the easy part. Soaring demand has dropped failure rates to the single digits. When the rare craft business folds, its equipment and facilities are often worth more than when they were purchased new. And then there is the pleasure quotient. Craft offers a lifestyle that is fun, even sexy, with laudable enviro-farm-to-table cache. "There is so much activity, more investment money, venture capital, big time investors. All kinds of business plans," says Brewers Association president Charlie Papazian.

Politicians are eager to support these dreams. There has been a spike in Small Business Administration loans for craft breweries. In 2009, there were 25 SBA brewery loans with a total value of $8 million compared to 245 SBA brewery loans in 2014 worth $90 million. States and local economic development authorities seek out craft beverage projects to promote tourism and support nearby small businesses. There has also been a flowering of companies lending money through equipment leases. Banks are making it easier to secure loans. And private investors are eager to sign up, with Wall Street venture funds circling around the larger, more ambitious projects. New online platforms are providing crowdsourcing financing for craft startups.

"Money is chasing people who are well connected in craft beer. Money is no longer a problem," says professor emeritus Michael Lewis of the University of California, Davis. "The tech sector is putting money in brewing. It will be hard to get the returns on investment they expect, but that isn't stopping them.

"The venture capital money is the most dangerous money out there," Lewis says. "They want a fast return on whatever they invest in. They have no understanding of the passion of brewing. They just want to make money." The smart money coming into the craft beer business, says Lewis, is committed to the beer making process, product, and profession. There are people who intend to remain owners."

So much easy money has, in many ways, raised the bar for starting a new craft venture. Because it is easier to quickly launch a substantial production facility, there is pressure to do nothing less. The typical new brewery project is larger, more expensive, and on a faster schedule than ever before. These projects require more business

tip

Invest your own energy and resources right from the start. By taking care with each small aspect of your business, you not only learn the ropes—you gain an intimate connection to your business. "My advice is to start as small as you can. Grow organically. Hand-label your bottles. Make your mistakes while you are small with less to lose. You will work harder, for longer hours, face more physical labor and be more passionate. You will have no cushion. This weeds out the people who weren't meant to be brewers," says Papazian, who admits to being wistful for the slower, earlier days of the craft beer revolution.

and technical expertise, according to equipment manufacturers. While it can be done for less, the typical cost of opening a new brewery has risen to between $500,000 and $1 million. Distilleries, as well, are starting larger, and there is a better understanding of the costs associated with aging the more popular whiskeys and bourbons, which adds to upfront capital costs of $1 million or more. Creating a hard cider brand is cheap by comparison, costing less than $300,000.

"You can start a brewery on $150,000 capital investment, if you don't pay yourself and are willing to scrounge around for equipment," says Brewers Association's Papazian. "It is more comfortable for a small-scale brewer to start with $500,000. The most successful start with $250,000. Their costs are low. They recoup their investment faster and grow more slowly."

The trick, then and now, is to raise enough money to buy the equipment and time necessary to succeed, yet to not sell so much of the venture that investors gain control. Each project pencils out to a different tipping point. Veteran brewers and distillers caution against grandiose plans that rely on significant, immediate sales to pay off high capital costs. There is no quick money in craft, they say.

In 2008, Tom Potter, cofounder of New York Distilling Company (http://thehoochlife. com) and a former partner in Brooklyn Brewery, could see that the fledgling craft distilling industry would follow a trajectory similar to craft beer. "We initially raised $1 million to launch NYDC. We've raised more since then, in a few additional rounds, but that was about the right amount to get going," says Potter. "The largest initial purchase was the custom-made still by CARL in Germany and related equipment, which cost about $500,000. That cost doesn't include fitting out the distillery space, which was more than double the cost of the still."

Potter took advantage of New York's Farm Distillery License, which allows on-premise sale and tasting rooms if the majority of the ingredients used come from New York state. This also cut their license fees and provided financial support to the venture. Still, it took two and a half years to get their first products, a trio of gins, to market. Considered one of the best business brains in the craft business, Potter and his partners—son Bill Potter and celebrated mixologist Allen Katz—sell their spirits at The Shanty, their popular bar in the Brooklyn distillery that stocks hundreds of spirits in addition to their own. They remain in control of their now-thriving business with their first aged whiskey—a rye aged with rock candy, known as Mister Katz's Rock & Rye—released in October 2014.

Self-Financing

It is a dream to own a craft company without having to sell some of it to outside investors, albeit a nightmare during the startup years. "I make beer because I love it. To pay the rent,

I'm a consultant for retailers and builders," says Evan Weinberg, 34, owner of Cismontaine Brewery (www.cismontanebrewing.com) in Rancho Santa Margarita, California. "I've been focused on the brewery for the last three years, and I took home $12,000 a year. Now I have to go back to work for a while as a consultant to make some money so I can continue making beer."

The goal is to find ways to make more beer without spending more money. Efficiency is illusive when you are undercapitalized, says Weinberg. And now he's also launched a distillery to make brandy. The capital costs are a heavy burden.

Weinberg built Cismontaine with personal savings, cash flow from the brewery, and a few bank loans. "It's small. We built it gradually," he says, noting he produces 2,500 barrels a year. "We make money, but it's tight." His initial investment was $130,000; adding in subsequent capital costs, his total investment adds up to $500,000 over five years. That's the minimum cost of getting started today, and it goes up to $1 million. "We see people throwing down $5 million, $6 million before they open their doors. Real money is being spent now.

"Our goal is to get the brewery and distillery to the place where we can live off the business, (we would probably need to produce 8,000 barrels/year from the brewery). It will take us another two years to get there. Will we do better if we get bigger? I don't know. If I were rich, I'd just pay for everything and be done already. You can fail if you don't make enough beer, and you can fail if you make too much. We try to stay just a tiny bit ahead of demand and grow slowly."

Garage operations financed out of the producer's back pocket still work, if you are patient and enjoy all-nighters in your garage. This slow, arduous path is how plenty of today's rising craft stars got started. If living hand-to-mouth doesn't drive you crazy, you may sell enough product to cover the cost of the invaluable education and gain enough credibility to raise some real money and build a proper production facility.

You will get to that next step if you spend your money making the best damn product you can. Develop a circle of repeat customers who know you and, more important, like you. Be the only place that makes what you make. Not everyone will want what you sell, but everyone who likes it will have to come to you to get it.

aha!

If you have a job that pays your bills with enough left over to slowly expand your craft hobby, you can self-finance a nano-brewery, micro-distillery, or small cidery. It's inexpensive to build something tiny. If you have a partner who can do the same, you are twice as likely to succeed.

Personal Balance Sheet

Assets		Totals
Cash and Checking		
Savings Accounts		
Real Estate/Home		
Automobiles		
Bonds		
Securities		
Insurance Cash Values		
Other		
Total Assets	A	$

Liabilities		Totals
Current Monthly Bills		
Credit Card/Charge Account Bills		
Mortgage		
Auto Loans		
Finance Company Loans		
Personal Debts		
Other		
Total Liabilities	B	$
Net Worth (A–B=C)	C	$

Degree of Indebtedness		
Total Liabilities	B	$
Total Assets	A	$
Degree of Indebtedness (B–A=D)		
	D	$

Note: If total liabilities exceed total assets, subtract assets from liabilities to determine degree of indebtedness (B–A=D).

FIGURE 7–1: **Personal Balance Sheet**

By filling out a personal balance sheet, you will be able to determine your net worth. Finding out your net worth is an important early step in the process of becoming a business owner because you need to find out what assets are available to you for investment in your business. This is a good step to take when you are trying to hammer out the financing details of your craft business.

Equipment Leasing

Equipment leasing is an easy way for a self-financed craft producer to expand. You can get the new equipment you want even when you don't have the credit history to get a bank to lend you the money. The equipment guarantees the loan, so there is little to lose.

The retained value of brewery, distillery, and cidery equipment is the secret, says Rick Wehner, with Brewery Finance (www.breweryfinance.com), a division of Pinnacle Capital Partners. "All the craft producers need similar, big-price-tag equipment, and we work with them all. Banks understand real estate more than equipment, and they certainly don't understand the value of this equipment on the secondary market. This equipment retains its value. We know where the industry is going and so we're willing to accept greater risk. We're easier to work with than a bank."

With a personal guarantee from the purchaser, Wehner finances 100 percent of the invoice for terms of two to five years at rates that are above bank rates but less expensive than bringing in equity investors, he says. For a big project with someone who has extensive experience and a track record with Brewery Finance, the rate can be as low as 5 percent. For someone new to craft with a questionable credit history, the rate can rise to 30 percent. Nine years ago, Wehner had this market to himself. Now, there are several equipment lenders specializing in craft.

Equipment leasing companies are flush, and you are not. Get them to compete for your business. The burgeoning field of equipment leasing opens the opportunity to negotiate rates. To help you get a handle on how equipment costs play a role in your startup and ongoing budgets, try using the two cost worksheets in Figure 7–2 on pages 103 and 104.

Investors

Outside investors are the most common form of financing a craft business. The first step toward approaching investors is to create a compelling investor packet that tells a story powerful enough to convince strangers that the business will succeed. A formal, well-produced presentation (in both print and electronic form) covers the high points of the business plan and explains the size of the raise and plans for spending the funds. Financial projections for the business and an analysis of the market and the competition should be included.

Beer, spirits, and cider are products that, in most cases, can be demonstrated. Show investors what they are buying. Let them taste at least a reasonable facsimile of what the company will make. Be prepared to answer any questions about process, ingredients, government incentives, taxes, and pending regulatory changes that could affect the

Startup Capital Requirements
One-Time Startup Expenses

Startup Expenses	Description	Amount
Advertising	Promotion for opening the business	
Starting inventory	Amount of inventory required to open	
Building construction	Amount per contractor bid and other costs	
Cash	Amount needed for the cash register	
Decorating	Estimate based on bid, if appropriate	
Deposits	Check with utility companies	
Fixtures and equipment	Use actual bids	
Insurance	Bid from insurance agent	
Lease payments	Fees to be paid before opening	
Licenses and permits	Check with city or state offices	
Miscellaneous	All other costs	
Professional fees	Include CPA, attorney, etc.	
Remodeling	Use contractor bids	
Rent	Fee to be paid before opening	
Services	Cleaning, accounting, etc.	
Signs	Use contractor bids	
Supplies	Office, cleaning, etc.	
Unanticipated expenses	Include an amount for the unexpected	
Other		
Other		
Total Startup Costs		$

FIGURE 7–2: **Startup Costs Worksheet**

These two worksheets will help you compute your initial cash requirements for your business. They list the things you need to consider when determining your startup costs and include both the one-time initial expenses to open your doors and the ongoing costs you'll face during the first 90 days.

Startup Capital Requirements
Ongoing Monthly Expenses*

Startup Expenses	Description	Amount
Advertising		
Bank service fees		
Credit card charges		
Delivery fees		
Dues and subscriptions		
Insurance	Exclude amount on preceding page	
Interest		
Inventory	See ** below	
Lease payments	Exclude amount on preceding page	
Loan payments	Principal and interest payments	
Office expenses		
Payroll other than owner		
Payroll taxes		
Professional fees		
Rent	Exclude amount on preceding page	
Repairs and maintenance		
Sales tax		
Supplies		
Telephone		
Utilities		
Your salary	Only if applicable during the first three months	
Other		
Total Ongoing Costs		$
Total Startup Costs	**Amount from preceding page**	$
Total Cash Needed		$

*Include the first three months' cash needs unless otherwise noted.

**Include amount required for inventory expansion. If inventory is to be replaced from cash sales, do not include here. Assume sales will generate enough cash for replacements.

FIGURE 7–2: **Startup Costs Worksheet,** continued

▶ I Love Los Angeles!

Ted Fourticq, a principal with Hancock Park Associates (www.hpcap.com), a Los Angeles-based private equity firm, wrote his master's thesis on the beer business a decade ago and decided now is the time to follow his beer muse. He is building a 5,000-square-foot brewery, taproom, and performance venue in Goleta, a beach town west of Santa Barbara. "This is a personal investment, not through the firm," he says. "The business plan doesn't look anything like the companies the firm invests in. This is for fun.

"The Los Angeles area has lagged [behind] the rest of the state on craft breweries. There is opportunity here," he says. With childhood friends—a pro surfer/filmmaker, a beer distributor, and the record producer/manager of singer Jack Johnson—Fourticq hopes to launch M Special Brewing Company in 2015. "We considered contract brewing. It's how Jim Koch did it. But real beer people reject it, and there can be quality-control issues. We are spending a little more up front to make sure it is done right," Fourticq says, without disclosing the budget. "We're set up to produce 5,000 barrels to start with, but have room to grow" in a space that costs $5,000 a month to rent.

The M Special prospectus says the plan is to "remake" the classic American lager favored by the 90 percent of beer drinkers who haven't yet switched from Bud and Miller. "Handmade, small batch," the prospectus says, "without the crap ingredients that the majors put in their beers."

business. Develop a list of potential investors and learn as much as possible about their interests and concerns before making contact. If they invest, they will have a say in how the company functions. Treating them with respect from the start sets a tone that facilitates cooperation. Have experienced legal and professional advisors on the project team before setting any meetings with potential investors.

A Word of Caution

The downside of selling part of a craft business to investors is well illustrated by the story of Balcones Distilling (www.balconesdistilling.com), Chip Tate's Waco, Texas, whiskey venture. Launched in 2008 by Tate and two partners, it took nearly a year to collect, and in some cases fabricate, the still and other equipment. But from the moment Tate released his first bottle of Baby Blue, a whiskey made from roasted Hopi blue corn that tastes like corn tortillas, sales soared. Tate released a single malt whiskey to similar acclaim. To keep up with demand, he needed money to expand.

Enter Gregory S. Allen in November 2013. For a reported $8.5 million, the Virginia businessman brought out Tate's partners and paid off the distillery's debts to take a majority stake in the venture. Tate's ownership was reduced to 27 percent, but he remained in charge of production and management of the distillery, which was producing 5,000 bottles of spirits a month, according to a *New York Times* December 27, 2014, article.

The honeymoon was short with the relationship souring as cost estimates for a new distillery rose from an early guess of $4 million to a more considered $8 million, then to the dream of $12 million. Things were said in anger. Cooperation ended. And by August 2014, the Allen-led Balcones board had suspended Tate and obtained a restraining order barring him from the distillery.

In mid-November, it appeared that Tate would triumph when a state judge ruled that the board had overstepped its authority. But the relationship was irreparably damaged. Before the end of the year, Tate and Allen had settled, with the founder selling his stake in Balcones and leaving the company. He is prohibited from starting a competing distillery for a year and a half.

"Investors want what you are and then get frustrated with what that actually means," says James Rodewald, author of *American Spirit*. "Chip is the wrong person if you want quick returns. He cares too much."

Private Equity

Private equity investors also made plenty of headway in 2014. Uinta Brewing Company in Salt Lake City, Utah, sold a majority share to Riverside Company. Sweetwater Brewing Company in Atlanta, Georgia, sold equity to TSG Consumer Partners. And Southern Tier Brewing Company in Lakewood, New York, sold a stake to Ulysses Management. After Ulysses announced its deal with Southern Tier, Steve Hindy of Brooklyn Brewery says, "the first thing they did was to bring in their own CEO. Founders are important to the culture and values of a craft business. It will be interesting to see if that straight business approach will work. Having a lot of money wasn't an advantage in the 1980s. New Amsterdam overbuilt. Pyramid went public and got ahead of demand and had to sell. We're planning a 1-million-barrel brewery we hope to build on Staten Island. We get calls from private equity folks on a daily basis offering to invest. It started in early 2014. They are looking for a five-year payout of their investment, quick multiples. They aren't long-term, patient investors."

The form of craft financing that gets a consistent thumbs down from established craft producers is private equity/venture financing, or whatever you want to call wealthy investment funds with notoriously short attention spans. Craft requires patience, and these folks have none.

But if you are in financial trouble—you expanded too fast and can't keep up with the debt payments or you can't keep up with demand and are burned out from trying—these bad boys start to look good. Few craft producers, however, stick around after the sale. And there is probably a reason for that.

Institutions

Banks are more open to craft than ever before, but they are most likely to respond to existing customers with a solid track record for paying obligations. Otherwise, be prepared to document a history of sound financial performance, show personal investment in the project, and provide collateral to assert your creditworthiness.

State Support

The trend in states is to offer more support for craft producers. Each state is different, and each county within each state will administer that state's programs in specific ways. First, contact the state guild. They make it their business to stay up to date on these programs. Talk to other producers in the state and ask for advice. Here are some examples of state programs fledgling craft breweries have accessed.

Zero Gravity Craft Brewery (www.zerogravitybeer.com), a Burlington, Vermont, craft brewery, received a $440,000 Vermont Economic Development Authority loan in the fall of 2014 to partially fund expansion into a full-scale production brewery. In a press release, the state cited the addition of nine employees over three years as the rationale for the loan. "Zero Gravity has been producing and selling award-winning beer since 2005 as a brewpub connected to the American Flatbread restaurant located in downtown Burlington. This will allow the company to expand its production capacity of Zero Gravity-brand craft beers and add a retail shop with tasting room and beer garden. The People's United Bank is also participating in the project," the authority stated in the release.

Denizens Brewing Company (http://denizensbrewingco.com) opened a 15-barrel brewery in a 7,500-square-foot space in downtown Silver Spring, Maryland, in 2014 with the help of a $500,000 bank loan from Eagle Bank backed by the Maryland Industrial Development Financing Authority, a Department of Business and Economic Development initiative.

Virginia Beer Company (www.virginiabeerco.com) owners Chris Smith and Robby Willey appealed to the tourism ambitions of the York County overseers of Williamsburg,

Virginia, when they were looking for a place to house their new brewery. As the third brewer in the region, perhaps Virginia Beer would provide the critical mass necessary for a local "spirits trail." That was enough to inspire the county economic development authority to write a $43,000 check to help open the brewery and taproom for the summer 2015 tourist season. Even though they had already raised $1.3 million from friends and family, every little bit helps. The county fathers instituted regulatory reforms that gave craft breweries, distillers, and cideries special status as engines for economic growth.

Crowdfunding Rewards Programs

Craft breweries, in particular, regularly raise funds through Kickstarter—an online service that allows you to ask strangers as well as friends, who read your plans on the Kickstarter (www.kickstarter.com) site, to support your dreams. They aren't, however, raising investment funds. These supporters earn "rewards" for financing your dreams. The campaigns are marketing opportunities paid for by the target audience. With a successful Kickstarter campaign, a craft producer can demonstrate the strength of its brand and identify its best customers, both of which are difficult to produce in other ways.

Three successful brewery Kickstarter campaigns were for projects that were already fully funded. Braxton Brewing Company (www.braxtonbrewing.com) of Greater Cincinnati set a Kickstarter brewery record in November 2014, raising $71,885 from 654 supporters in 34 hours, substantially exceeding its $30,000 target to fund the "Taproom of the Future." The brewer surpassed previous record holders Kittery, Maine's Tributary Brewing Company (http://tributarybrewingcompany.com) with $65,565, and San Diego-based Modern Times Beer (http://moderntimesbeer.com) at $65,471.

The rewards for participants in those campaigns were designed to deepen existing relationships. For instance, $50 bought Modern Times backers a 90-minute webinar explaining how the brewery started, along with the business plan, budget, fundraising strategy, brewery design, licensing, and more. The three companies capitalized on the connections with their devoted fans by communicating frequently and thoughtfully, keeping their backers up to date on the project. Other tips: Set realistic fulfillment schedules to avoid the possibility of disappointing participants. After all, fulfillment is completely up to the fundraiser.

> **fun fact** ☺
>
> Sites like Kickstarter do not fall under securities laws (although the income is taxable). But there are limits to the premiums. Most states will not allow alcoholic beverages to be given away, and you cannot sell them without a license.

A word of caution: Kickstarter can also damage a brand. Wilderness Brewing Company in Kansas City, Missouri, raised more than $40,000 on Kickstarter in 2011 and has yet to launch. "Please believe me when I say that broken agreements, various ordinances, and dashed hopes are not an easy thing," wrote cofounder Mike Reinhardt in an August 2014 update to the campaign, in which he also apologized to frustrated backers for the delay.

Some 400 craft breweries have raised funds through Kickstarter. A study of Kickstarter craft brewery campaigns by CraftFund (http://craftfund.com), a firm specializing in crowdfunding, showed 29 successful campaigns out of 71 launched as of December 2012, for a 41 percent success rate. They produced an average of 231 donations per campaign, with an average donation of $96. The most money a brewery has crowdfunded (as of the end of 2014) was $71,000, and only a handful of campaigns have raised more than $30,000. Successful campaigns on average had a lower average target ($17,224) than unsuccessful campaigns ($24,730)." Video presentations and updates make the breweries' stories more compelling.

▶ Kickstarting a Brand

Profile of a successful Kickstarter craft rewards campaign by the Community and Economic Development program at the University of North Carolina School of Government:

With a population of 25,000, Asheboro, North Carolina, is a shrinking town desperate to generate jobs. In 2011, the city adopted a $12 million revitalization plan to turn the formerly "dry" town, where alcohol consumption was illegal until 2008, into a tourist destination. Local hobby brewers Joel McClosky and Andrew Deming seized the moment and proposed the town's first brewery, Four Saints Brewing Company (www.foursaintsbrewing.com). The financing of a brewery in a rural, recently dry town, run by two friends with no experience starting a business or commercially brewing beer, was considered too risky of an investment for the local banks or the town's redevelopment authority. So the partners turned to Kickstarter.

By then, food businesses had begun turning to Kickstarter to raise startup funds. Most were in much bigger, younger cities: the four most highly funded food businesses were in Brooklyn, Seattle, San Francisco, and Washington, DC. McClosky and Deming knew that the catchy videos, social media campaigns, and frantic pace that propel many projects to success on Kickstarter would not be the best way to successfully engage Randolph County residents.

Instead, they decided to run an offline, face-to-face campaign before beginning to actually raise money on the site. They also knew they would have to educate their potential "backers"—as

▶ **Kickstarting a Brand,** continued

those who donate to campaigns are known—about Kickstarter. The site may have had a buzz in Brooklyn and San Francisco, but it was not necessarily familiar to everyone they hoped to reach in Randolph County. Months before raising their first dollar, they were serving tastes of their beer at community events and guiding the conversation from stouts and ales to something bigger: a shared vision for not just their business, but for all of downtown Asheboro. To McClosky and Deming, beer could bring people together, and a downtown brewery could support the renaissance so many sought in Asheboro.

Four Saints' Kickstarter campaign launched on May 23, 2012, and ended 39 days later, raising $52,375—$7,000 over the goal and enough to make Four Saints the fifth most highly funded food business on Kickstarter at that time and one of the most highly funded breweries ever. While the partners knew that the community was interested in their brewery, a functioning brewery and tasting room would take more than $52,000 to open.

The initial money allowed McClosky and Deming to sign a lease, begin the licensing and permitting process, and purchase some commercial-grade brewing equipment. Importantly, the firm's crowdfunding success also got the attention of an angel investor. Four Saints received $100,000 in equity financing from an investor who increased that commitment to $150,000 in 2014. Four Saints leveraged this equity investment to secure a Small Business Administration-guaranteed commercial loan to supply its remaining capital needs.

Though the Four Saints case is a success story, they encountered challenges stemming from their many stakeholders' expectations. While crowdfunding can be a great way to create excitement and build momentum for a project, it typically takes advantage of a short timeframe, a sense of urgency, and frequent updates. This contrasts with the much slower pace of permitting, site selection, acquisition, and construction of a facility. More than two years after its campaign, construction of the downtown brewery and bar is not yet complete. They have had to push back their opening date more than once, and now expect to open in early 2015. For a business, this timeframe is not out of the ordinary. But for some backers of their campaign, the pace is surprising, and for a few, frustrating.

Four Saints' backers received only small "rewards" for their funds—T-shirts, bottle openers, and mugs, for example. Backers were funding the business for reasons that transcended personal financial gain.

Stone Brewing's Indiegogo (www.indiegogo.com/projects/stone-groundbreaking-collaborations--2) campaign in the summer of 2014 shattered all crowdfunding records, raising $2.5 million. In its first weeks, however, the campaign was a disaster. As originally conceived, the campaign was to raise funds to build the brewery's new Berlin, Germany, campus. For minimum support level of $40, fans would receive a special collaboration brew or a limited edition T-shirt, among other rewards. The prizes and price points escalated to $30,000 for a couple of lucky fans who bought a hot night on the town in San Diego, living life in Greg Koch's shoes. Many fans thought it was a cheesy way for America's 10th largest brewery to finance growth.

Koch reconceived the campaign as an "exclusive presales event," which he announced in an uncomfortable video apology where he thanked the 14,000 folks who had signed up and "trusted our ability to deliver something you will think is awesome." The mea culpa worked, and participation skyrocketed. Not only did Stone engage its own 400,000 strong social media network, the collaborations with other breweries engaged those breweries' fans as well. For each new release of a collaborative brew, Stone created a video telling the story of its creation, another opportunity to interact with fans. The campaign target of $1 million—along with the misfired launch—were soon forgotten.

Crowdfunding Equity Campaigns

One day you will be able to sell stock to investors using a form of crowdfunding; at least the legislation to enable that to happen—the 2012 federal JOBS Act—has passed Congress. Companies that meet certain requirements, including background checks, providing certain disclosures and audited financial statements, may be eligible to sell equity in their ventures online through an intermediary registered with the Securities and Exchange Commission. The online equity exchanges likely will work in ways similar to a Kickstarter campaign, only instead of receiving rewards for their money, investors will be buying shares in your craft company. You will have to treat them like other publicly traded companies treat their investors. Unfortunately, the SEC is not expected to release the specific rules and regulations setting up these online exchanges until late 2015. For now, the details of how this will work are locked in a black box at the SEC.

In the meantime, CraftFund, based in Milwaukee, Wisconsin, is taking advantage of that state's newly approved intrastate equity crowdsourcing law, working with breweries, distilleries, and craft food companies, categories the fund believes are best suited for equity crowdfunding. Wisconsin is the first of what David Dupee, founder of CraftFund, thinks will be many states to jump ahead of the SEC. "Many people worry that the federal rules, when they finally come out, won't be practical," he says, and states increasingly are moving forward on their own.

CraftFund launched a three-month equity crowdfunding offer in October to raise $250,000 to finance the expansion of Mob Craft, a year-old Wisconsin brewery. At the deadline for this book, the offering was still open. The size of investments ranged from the maximum of $10,000 to the minimum of $500. The average investment was $1,600. Wisconsin caps equity crowdfunding at $1 million. These kinds of offerings have the potential to turn customers into advocates by becoming owners, he says. Owning is more exciting than the now-ordinary rewards programs Kickstarter offers.

Travis Benoit, founder of CrowdBrewed (https://crowdbrewed.com), a New York City-based company that is a registered broker-dealer specializing in equity crowdfunding, expects an explosion of these kinds of financing deals when the SEC rules are released. "It will be the Wild West. With 2,000 breweries and hundreds of distilleries in the pipeline, everyone can raise small amounts of money from lots of people, and a few people will raise $1 million or more." The best candidates are the craft companies that are already in operation, Benoit says.

> ### tip
>
> "The long-term marketing potential of this pool of owners is huge. Beer is so competitive. This is a way to stand out," says Dupee. The best candidates for crowdsourced equity kind of funding have:
>
> - An easy-to-understand business plan;
> - A story that resonates emotionally with investors;
> - And a strong connection to their local communities.

Sell a Brand

Spirits are a brand-driven business. Consumers buy Maker's Mark without wondering who owns it (it's Japan's Suntory Corp.). It is possible for a craft distiller to build a brand and sell it without hurting either the brand or the other brands produced by your craft distillery. For a self-financed distillery or a closely held company, this creates opportunities that you may want to consider in your original business plan for a craft distillery. While a similar approach might be possible with craft beer, it has never been tried. The brewery itself and other ancillary businesses, such as a distribution company, are considered the salable assets.

When Alameda, California's legendary St. George Distillery sold its Hangar 1 Vodka to New Jersey-based Proximo Spirits, consumers didn't blink. The deal provided founder Jörg Rupf the cash he needed to retire and hand control of the distillery to his protégé

Lance Winters. Winters plans to soon introduce a new St. George brand of vodka that will compete with its former brand.

Proximo has been buying up craft brands to add to a portfolio that includes Jose Cuervo tequila. In addition to Hangar 1, it purchased Stranahan's Colorado Whiskey in December 2013. Beyond boilerplate statements about maintaining the standards set by the founders of these brands, the secretive private company refuses to speak about its craft spirits plans. By violating the key tenet of the craft creed of full disclosure, Proximo asks consumers to take it on faith that these brands will continue to be handmade, craft products, which is asking a lot.

That's not the case for Tuthilltown Distillery. In 2005, Ralph Erenzo opened the first stand-alone craft distillery in New York State, taking advantage of a new craft-specific license lowering fees from $50,000 to $1,450. His first Tuthilltown Spirits product was apple vodka, but he is best known for his Hudson Valley bourbons. In 2010, he surprised the craft spirits industry when he sold the bourbon brand to British liquor giant W. Grant & Sons, owners of Glenfiddich, Hendricks, and Stolichnaya.

The deal gave Erenzo access to Grant's international marketing and distribution system, and he's been able to expand production—a necessity because he will continue to make the Hudson Valley bourbons at least until 2017. He is allowed to create a new whiskey brand that he's aging for longer than the two-year Hudson Whiskeys as long as he doesn't release it until 2017.

"When W. Grant approached us, we didn't sell the whole place. It had been six years of our lives. They just bought Hudson," says Erenzo. "We continue to make every drop of it. They distribute it. It allowed us to expand from 10,000-proof gallons in 2012 to 60,000-proof gallons in 2013. There is a big export business. We thought if we could make a big splash in Paris, it would be easier to sell our whiskey here in America, and it was true. We are in every state now and around the world."

"The problem with partnering with a large company is they have a different mentality. They think in tens of thousands, and we think in hundreds. It's a whole different ball game. It is a case-by-case basis whether to team with a big guy. We only sold the brand, kept control of production.

"We had no experience when we started; there was no place to get it. So it took us three years and $750,000 to get up and running. Today, you need $1.5 million to $5 million to get started. The good news is banks are open to funding craft distilleries now."

tip

Erenzo offered this advice: Get help reviewing documents. Larger companies have teams of attorneys on their side. Have a qualified set of eyes reviewing documents for you, too.

Craft Buying Craft

Craft breweries, however, are starting to buy other craft breweries. Within the craft community, it is akin to a big brother putting his arm around a struggling sibling, at least, that is the case at this very early stage in this developing trend.

Green Flash Brewing's purchase in 2014 of Alpine Brew Company—both based in the San Diego region—was the first of these deals and follows Green Flash's announcement that it is building a new $20 million, 100,000-barrel brewery in Virginia Beach, Virginia, in 2016. "One of the reasons we bought them is their barrel-aged beer program," Green Flash cofounder Mike Hinkley says. "We will be able to plug Alpine's specialty beers in the national market. It is inevitable that craft brewers will combine. With all the competition, new people in the beer business don't understand how long it takes to get established. It takes a long time."

Selling to an Industrial Beer or Spirits Company

Nothing gets craft producers' knickers in a knot faster than the idea of selling out to industrial producers. Anheuser-Busch's ongoing craft brewery buying spree is a particular existential crisis that, to many in the craft movement, threatens the very definition of craft beer. A network of craft breweries owned by Busch? Yikes! The anti-Budweiser folks do not know what to do when their friends and fellow craft brewers join forces with the enemy. While they understand the allure of these big, never-before-seen paydays for craft brewers, taking the bait is treason and represents the end of an era when there was a clear delineation between the bad- and the good-beer guys.

In 2014, the big news in craft beer was Anheuser-Busch InBev's $50 million purchase of 10 Barrel Brewing, a 45,000-barrel Bend, Oregon, brewery with three brewpubs, and the equally rich purchase of Elysian Brewing Company, at 50,000-barrel Seattle brewery with four brewpubs. These deals followed the big beer company's $25 million purchase of Blue Point Brewing, a Long Island-based brewery producing 60,000 barrels a year (figures are according to industry analysts). In 2011, Anheuser-Busch InBev bought Chicago's 100,000-barrel/year Goose Island Beer Company for $39 million, after which the founders left the company.

The management of these newly purchased craft companies have generally remained in place, assuring their fans, as the founders of 10 Barrel did, that these deals are about expanding, not selling out. Those assurances did little to calm 10 Barrel's fans, who took to social media to lambast the owners. Talk swirled about the "corporatization" of the craft beer movement now that it was clear Anheuser-Busch was embarking on a national strategy to buy regional craft brands.

► Manage Your Margins

In general, according to IBISWorld analyses of the financial health of the craft brewery sector: Profit margins vary considerably depending on the size of the brewery and its ability to distribute products regionally. On average, profit margins—earnings before interest and taxes—are expected to average 9.1 percent across the industry in 2015. Industry establishments have benefited from substantial increases in demand for craft beers during the past five years, which has allowed operators to charge higher prices and produce much more volume.

The largest costs to breweries are purchases of raw materials, which IBISWorld estimates that, on an industry-wide basis, the cost of raw materials will account for 38.5 percent of total industry revenues in 2015. These raw materials include packaging materials such as glass, aluminum and corrugated cardboard. Packaging costs have increased significantly over the past five years, particularly aluminum cans, due to commodity prices rising.

Each brewer's recipe differs depending on the type of beer made, which creates some differences in the level of purchases across firms. Over the five years to 2020, craft beers are expected to become immensely popular and will likely lead to ingredient suppliers increasingly choosing to issue supplier contracts to the industry's producers. As the availability of key inputs such as malt and hops becomes increasingly strained, industry costs may increase going forward.

Labor represents a relatively small portion of industry revenue, accounting for about 4 percent of industry revenue in 2015. The ratio of wages to revenue has declined during the five years to 2015 from 5.5 percent in 2010. Over the five years to 2020, more demand for craft brews is expected to lead to additional employment in the industry, but both revenue growth and purchases of capital are expected to outpace wage increases.

Depreciation varies considerably depending on the size of the brewery and type of equipment used. In 2015, average depreciation is estimated to be 2.8 percent of revenue. Generally, beer brewing is considered a capital-intensive process and depreciation of plants and equipment is significant. Depreciation is not forecast to fluctuate dramatically over the five years to 2020, although increasing purchases of equipment will necessitate additional accounting for depreciation expenses.

The industry incurs a significant amount of local, state and federal taxes, administrative expenses and legal costs. Licensing, health audits, and labeling requirements by the TTB, BAFTE, FDA and local governments contribute to the industry's large regulatory expenses. Marketing expenses are estimated to average 4.2 percent of total revenues on an industry wide basis in 2015.

Speaking to craft beer trade publication Brewpublic (http://brewpublic.com), Anheuser-Busch's executive in charge of its new craft brands, Andy Goeler, said there is no "grand strategy." Rather, the world's largest beer company is being "opportunistic." The company will be expanding these brands quickly. "It is crazy for us [ABI] to buy something like this and to come in and change or mess up," Goeler says. "It just makes no sense. We have no plan at all to do anything like that. It defeats the whole purpose of why we bought it."

"There's a lot of shock right now, for sure," says 10 Barrel founder Garrett Wales. "The beer audience in the Northwest is incredibly passionate. What we are asking for is for the people to let the beer do the talking. We're saying a lot of things that sound really promising and so are our partners at Anheuser-Busch, and it's going to come true. I think right now a lot of people are thinking, 'Lies, lies, lies! Spin! Spin! Spin!' but we are still involved in the company. The brewers are still involved in the company. The same thing is going to keep on happening. Just let the beer do the talking. That's all we're asking from people."

warning

For new people coming into craft, there will be increased opportunity as well as competition. Consumers who pride themselves on avoiding industrial beer may become disenchanted with these "sellout" craft brands and be open to trying something new. But beware. With access to the deep pockets of giant companies, these "sellout" brands will be able to fight for those customers by spending more money on marketing. Keeping up will be costly.

Also in 2014, Founders Brewing Company (http://foundersbrewing.com), based in Michigan, sold a 30 percent stake to Spain's largest brewery, Mahou San Miguel (www.mahou-sanmiguel.com) for as much as $90 million, according to industry sources. The sale comes during a period of rapid growth—multiple years of 75 percent annual growth in sales—fueled by the popularity of its low-alcohol All-Day IPA. A recently launched expansion project will increase Founders' capacity from the current 207,000 barrels a year to an estimated 900,000 barrels. According to the craft brewery, the sale to Mahou San Miguel enables it to offer investors a chance to capitalize on their investment and expand the brand. Mahou San Miguel produced more than 10.4 million barrels of beer in 2012 with revenues exceeding $1.4 billion.

The deals have forced a discussion within the craft brewers' trade association, Brewers Association, about the definition of who is and is not a craft brewer. BA does not define 10 Barrel, Blue Point, Goose Island, and Founders as "craft" because they sold more than a 25 percent interest to a noncraft alcoholic beverage industry member. However, companies that sold more than 25 percent stakes to nonbeer interests continue to be members of the BA.

Gaining Traction in a Crowded Market

F rosty ice climbers on a mountain pick axe their way through a frozen waterfall and emerge in a rowdy bar, heroes with ice-cold beers in hand. Crest-fallen couch potatoes watching their team fumble a football game light up as the pretty, smartest-person-in-the-room arrives with ice-cold beers in hand. Svelte young beauties strolling on the beach with ice cold beers. The world's most interesting man pours a, you guessed it, ice cold beer. The world's biggest beer companies spend $1 billion a year on this cast of characters to do one thing . . . and it is not to convince Americans to drink more beer.

Budweiser, Coors, Corona, Dos Equis, and other big beer brands use TV ads to try to convince each other's fans to switch brands. They have been doing this for decades, grabbing and losing slivers of what is now a fast shrinking group of old fashioned beer drinkers. And yet, these multinational behemoths continue year after year to sell the fantasy of drinking really cold beverages to gain friends, have sex, and become a mock-sophisticate.

Jim Koch's Boston Beer is the only craft beer company to ever launch a TV ad campaign. His early efforts using humor and sex appeal failed. Now he sells the taste of Sam Adams beer, an inside look at the traditional beer-making process and the difference high-quality ingredients make in beer. He sells to a smart audience that values authenticity.

The rest of the craft breweries take pride in not advertising to mass audiences. Sierra Nevada's Ken Grossman claims to have never bought a mass-market ad. Period. No national magazines, newspapers, or television. He likes the personal touch, local media outlets reaching local beer drinkers. To open his second Sierra Nevada brewery in Ashland, North Carolina, in 2014, Grossman organized an elaborate summer-long bus tour across the country, staging a string of beer festivals, and all along the way he joined his friends at their craft breweries to brew limited production cooperative beers. The festivals and one-off beers demonstrated the camaraderie within the craft community and brought craft fans together to drink lots of craft beer.

It also "almost killed me," says Grossman. It took an enormous amount of time and energy on the part of the Sierra Nevada staff and, in the end, celebrated hard-core fans while ignoring the 90 percent of America that doesn't drink craft beer. Grossman swears he will never do anything like it again. And yet he still maintains his no-mass-marketing dictum.

Push will soon come to shove at Sierra Nevada and every other large craft brewery. They built their fanbase by handing curious people beers that tasted nothing like the beers they'd had before. Those folks told their friends about these wonderful new beers and, one by one, the craft beer audience grew. And then it stalled, and the flat line stretched to the dawn of social media in the mid-2000s. "The industry came alive with social media," says David Walker, cofounder of Walker Firestone Brewery. "It was a true multiplier." The explosion in craft beer popularity continues to grow as a new generation of fans share their craft discoveries more easily with more friends.

They may not realize it yet, but the national craft brands will take the next step up the marketing ladder and create national mass-market advertising campaigns. Founders like

Grossman will hate it, but they have no choice but to follow Koch's lead if they want to keep growing. "Craft has momentum in a flat beer market because there is a generation of transformed palates," Craft Brew Alliance CEO Andy Thomas told a recent Brewbound conference. Now, craft needs to grow up and start acting like the beer market leader it is. "We need to reach beer drinkers in grocery stores, convenience stores, Costco, and Walmart. We need a national footprint." To those who disdain Big Beer's flashy television ads, Thomas says, "We have to be involved in shaping the future of beer. You are the stewards of the beer industry identity of tomorrow."

Boston Beer's Koch "swore he would never sell Sam Adams in a can," says Lester Jones, chief economist for the National Beer Wholesalers Association. But when he wanted to have his beers on airplanes, in airports and convenience stores and outdoor events, he put Sam Adams in a can. Sierra Nevada is an outdoor brand and, naturally, the company sponsors hiking, biking, and wilderness events. "Cans are the superior package for an outdoor beer," he says. But the company refused to offer their beer in cans until the last couple of years. Now, its 12-pack of cans is a big seller in the craft category. "It's the most significant thing they have done" to support the brand, he says.

The craft guys started a revolution in beer. They've been aggressive, says Joe Thompson, a mergers and acquisitions consultant who often represents larger brewers and distributors. "Wholesalers fought back, but craft is winning. In the last five years, wholesalers and retailers have spent more time and attention on the craft category and taken time and attention away from Budweiser and Miller. Craft is eating Big Beer alive.

"Now that the big companies have lost enough volume, they are turning their big guns at the craft category. They are smart. They will use their scale to go after the craft business and price aggressively," says Thompson. Expect many more purchases of craft brands by the multi-national beer giants that respond to consumer demand for "local" products.

The big craft players are going to have to fight to keep growing. And those that have enjoyed being in a category that has done nothing but grow with consumers flocking

> **tip** ⓘ
>
> Don't be shy about making a little noise about your brew. "How brewers support their brands in the marketplace is critical to a distributor's ability to sell that brand," says Lester Jones with the National Beer Wholesalers Association. "Knowing that a brewer is doing something to support the brand, putting money into any type of advertising, makes sales to retailers so much easier. Wouldn't your job be easier if there were ads for the beer you are selling playing on every TV in every bar you went into to sell that product?"

to them, will be tested, Thompson says. Survival will depend on marketing muscles craft has not yet developed. "The brewers making a couple hundred thousand barrels will be fine, and the little bitty guys will be fine. In between is going to be a tough environment. Thirty-six percent of beer is drunk by 22- to 34-year-olds, and only 2 percent of that group is loyal to a brand."

Keith Lemcke, vice president of Chicago-based Siebel Institute of Technology and marketing manager for the World Brewing Academy, says marketing is now a dedicated position at even the smallest breweries and distilleries. "This person operates effective social media, trains sales staff in stores, trains bartenders, and grocery store workers. You have to have a marketing person from the start with an effective approach. Price competition is creeping in among the bigger craft brewers. You have to be prepared to respond." In other words, be ready to sell your brand and pivot your message on a dime.

> **tip**
> Make marketing a priority. "Craft beer no longer sells itself," says University of California, Davis, professor emeritus Michael Lewis. "It's harder and more expensive to sell your beer. At least 25 percent of your budget will go to marketing."

What Is Branding, Exactly?

Let's take a look at the basics of branding, courtesy of the expert branders themselves, the team at Entrepreneur. They will walk you through the basics of branding in the next three sections ("What is Branding, Exactly?," "Building a Branding Strategy," and "Bringing It All Together.")

Branding is a very misunderstood term. Many people think of branding as just advertising or a really cool-looking logo, but it's much more complex—and much more exciting, too.

▶ *Branding is your company's foundation.* Branding is more than an element of marketing, and it's not just about awareness, a trademark, or a logo. Branding is your company's reason for being, the synchronization of everything about your company that leads to consistency for you as the owner, your employees, and your potential customers. Branding meshes your marketing, public relations, business plan, packaging, pricing, customers, and employees.

▶ *Branding creates value.* If done right, branding makes the buyer trust and believe your product is somehow better than those of your competitors. Generally, the more distinctive you can make your brand, the less likely the customer will be willing to use another company's product or service, even if yours is slightly

> ## ▶ Top 15 New Craft Beer Brands Released in 2014–Supermarket Sales
>
> 1. Samuel Adams Rebel IPA—$21,116,309
>
> 2. Sierra Nevada variety pack—$11,374,208
>
> 3. New Belgium Snapshot Wheat—$4,530,783
>
> 4. Deschutes Fresh Squeezed IPA—$3,065,053
>
> 5. Stone Go To IPA—$2,019,261
>
> 6. New Belgium Special Release—$753,641
>
> 7. Sierra Nevada Beer Camp Across America—$722,419
>
> 8. Anchor IPA—$698,488
>
> 9. Dogfish Head Namaste Witbier—$667,338
>
> 10. Cigar City Invasion Pale Ale—$542,432
>
> 11. Ommegang Game of Thrones Fire and Blood—$423,127
>
> 12. Ommegang Game of Thrones Valar Morghulis—$414,994
>
> 13. Small Town Not Your Father's Root Beer—$413,540
>
> 14. Ballast Point Grapefruit Sculpin IPA—$378,418
>
> 15. Rhinegeist Truth IPA—$363,303
>
> *Source*: IRI supermarket sales data, released March 2015

more expensive. "Branding is the reason why people perceive you as the only solution to their problem," says Rob Frankel, a branding expert and author of *The Revenge of Brand X: How to Build a Big Time Brand on the Web or Anywhere Else*. "Once you clearly can articulate your brand, people have a way of evangelizing your brand."

▶ *Branding clarifies your message.* You have less money to spend on advertising and marketing as a startup entrepreneur, and good branding can help you direct your money more effectively. "The more distinct and clear your brand, the harder your advertising works," Frankel says. "Instead of having to run your ads eight or nine times, you only have to run them three times."

▶ *Branding is a promise.* At the end of the day, branding is the simple, steady promise you make to every customer who walks through your door—today, tomorrow, and ten years from now. Your company's ads and brochures might say you offer speedy, friendly service, but if customers find your service slow and surly, they'll walk out the door feeling betrayed. In their eyes, you promised something that you didn't deliver, and no amount of advertising will ever make up for the gap between what your company says and what it does. Branding creates the consistency that allows you to deliver on your promise over and over again.

Building a Branding Strategy

Your business plan should include a branding strategy. This is your written plan for how you'll apply your brand strategically throughout the company over time.

At its core, a good branding strategy lists the one or two most important elements of your product or service, describes your company's ultimate purpose in the world, and defines your target customer. The result is a blueprint for what's most important to your company and to your customer.

Don't worry; creating a branding strategy isn't nearly as scary or as complicated as it sounds. Here's how:

▶ *Step one*. Set yourself apart. Why should people buy from you instead of the same kind of business across town? Think about the intangible qualities of your product or service, using adjectives from "friendly" to "fast" and every word in between. Your goal is to own a position in the customer's mind so they think of you differently than the competition. "Powerful brands will own a word—like Volvo [owns] safety," says Laura Ries, an Atlanta marketing consultant and co-author of *The 22 Immutable Laws of Branding: How to Build a Product or Service into a World-Class Brand.* Which word will your company own? A new hair salon might focus on the adjective "convenient" and stay open a few hours later in the evening for customers who work late—something no other local salon might do. How will you be different from the competition? The answers are valuable assets that constitute the basis of your brand.

▶ *Step two*. Know your target customer. Once you've defined your product or service, think about your target customer. You've probably already gathered demographic information about the market you're entering, but think about the actual customers who will walk through your door. Who is this person, and what is the one thing he or she ultimately wants from your product or service? After all, the customer is buying it for a reason. What will your customer demand from you?

▶ *Step three*. Develop a personality. How will you show customers every day what you're all about? A lot of small companies write mission statements that say

▶ **Top Ten New Craft Vendors Selling in IRI Tracked Supermarkets**

The number of craft brands sold in supermarkets increased sharply in 2014, to 735 compared to 595 in 2013 and 484 in 2012.

1. Rhinegeist Brewery, Cincinnati, Ohio—$782,539
2. Griffin Claw Brewing Company, Birmingham, Michigan—$570,128
3. Small Town Brewery, Wauconda, Illinois—$413,540
4. Gilgamesh Brewing, Salem, Oregon—$304,454
5. Exile Brewing Company, Des Moines, Iowa—$264,785
6. Belching Beaver Brewery, Vista, California—$225,979
7. Old Bust Head Brewing Company, Warrenton, Virginia—$208,175
8. Everybodys Brewing, White Salmon, Washington—$177,344
9. Pisgah Brewing Company, Black Mountain, North Carolina—$132,695
10. Grapevine Craft Brewery, Farmers Branch, Texas—$131,133

Source: IRI

the company will "value" customers and strive for "excellent customer service." Unfortunately, these words are all talk, and no action. Dig deeper and think about how you'll fulfill your brand's promise and provide value and service to the people you serve. If you promise quick service, for example, what will "quick" mean inside your company? And how will you make sure service stays speedy? Along the way, you're laying the foundation of your hiring strategy and how future employees will be expected to interact with customers. You're also creating the template for your advertising and marketing strategy.

Your branding strategy doesn't need to be more than one page long at most. It can even be as short as one paragraph. It all depends on your product or service and your industry. The important thing is that you answer these questions before you open your doors.

Bringing It All Together

Congratulations—you've written your branding strategy. Now you'll have to manage your fledgling craft brand. This is when the fun really begins. Here are some tips:

▶ *Keep ads brand-focused*. Keep your promotional blitzes narrowly focused on your chief promise to potential customers. For example, a new brewery might see the open-view brewing/taproom as its greatest brand-building asset. Keep your message simple and consistent so people get the same message every time they see your name and logo.

▶ *Be consistent*. Filter every business proposition through a branding filter. How does this opportunity help build the company's brand? How does this opportunity fit our branding strategy? These questions will keep you focused and put you in front of people who fit your product or service.

▶ *Shed the deadweight*. Good businesses are willing to change their brands but are careful not to lose sight of their original customer base and branding message.

There's a lot of work that goes into launching and building a world-class brand, but it pays off. Think of your fledgling brand as a baby you have to nurture, guide, and shape every day so it grows up to be dependable, hardworking, and respectable in your customers' eyes. One day your company's brand will make you proud. But you'll have to invest the time, energy, and thought it takes to make that happen.

Getting Started

Now, you can apply that basic branding knowledge from Entrepreneur to the specific world of craft, accounting for the unique characteristics of this industry as you go.

You are entering a far more competitive sector than existed even five years ago. You must have a marketing strategy written into your business plan and that strategy has to be reflected in every decision you make. You are starting out behind many others. You will need to make a loud splash in the market to be heard above all the rest of the noise.

The old, slow way of selling beer by making great beer and gaining a solid following of people who want you to succeed still works, says BA's Papazian. "That following will get you through the difficult times when you have to take a leap and spend more to grow to get to the next level." And when you do spend money on marketing, it won't be to buy ads. "It is investing in an employee who is on the street talking to retailers, going to beer festivals, talking to beer drinkers, building relationships with distributors and restaurants."

Craft is personal. Craft is local. And craft fans still want to know who made the drink in their hand. Marketing a craft brand starts with understanding the founder's story, which is a very different thing than deciding what that story should be. Why is this product being made here and now? What brought the founder to this place? Where does the founder want to take this enterprise? Is it the founder's product, or is the brewmaster or distiller the soul of the brand? Answering these questions is an existential exercise that will ground the marketing in the company's greater mission. When logos, websites, signage, and T-shirts reflect that mission in authentic ways, there is an opportunity to engage the all-important Millennial consumer.

"The first thing we had to do when we opened was to explain the product to consumers," says Ralph Erenzo, founder of Hudson Valley's Tuthilltown Spirits in Gardiner, New York. "The best person to do that is the distiller. What do we make? Why and how, the full story. When I went out to talk with people in bars, it was the first time anyone had ever met the person who made the spirits they were drinking. We're going up against big brands with deep pockets and trying to push them aside on stores shelves. It is critical to be able to sell out of our tasting room where we have a face-to-face opportunity with the consumer. They walk out with a bottle, but they don't come back to us for the next one. They take it to their local retailer and ask for it. We have to be there, too."

To enhance the distillery experience for his customers, Erenzo is buying the gristmill next door to create a park so people can picnic when they visit. "It adds a tourist element. We want people to hang out, have lunch, throw rocks in the river, and experience our world."

You may not have a beautiful location, but you can—and must—create a virtual reality for your brand that is appealing, welcoming, and engaging. Everything you do online should be considered part of your virtual reality.

Websites should be designed with the same sense of place that defines the brewery, distillery, or cidery. It is often the first "place" customers interact with a craft brand. The founder's story should inform the look, feel, and messaging on the site, including the logo and product labels. When a website does not include photos of the founders or a sense of where the product is made, it is a lost opportunity to capture a critical selling point for craft and builds engagement with the brand.

Robust, thoughtful Facebook, Twitter, Instagram, and other social media programs—a minimum marketing effort for any craft brand—should be designed to drive customers to the website where guests have the opportunity to engage more deeply with the brand. Measuring that engagement is critical to knowing if the website is serving its purpose. How long do guests stay on the site? Google analytics provides average length of time on the site. How deeply did the guest engage with the brand? Google analytics provides average number of site "pages viewed."

No website is complete without providing fans with a way to stay connected to the brand. How many visitors "subscribe" when they visit the site? The list of subscribers is a valuable but fragile asset. Handled incorrectly, these fans will "unsubscribe" and be beyond reach. Offered engaging, relevant information and opportunities, they will share the brand's emails with friends. Subscribers are invited to events featuring the brand and are the people most likely to ask for the brand at stores, restaurants, and bars.

Your online world will be particularly important before you open your real-world doors. To cultivate customers before they opened their doors in 2013, McMinnville, Oregon's Grain Station Brew Works (http://grainstation.com) owners, Kelly McDonald and Mark Vickery, launched a "Community Supported Brewery Pubscription Plan." Think of a weekly delivery of produce from a CSA (Community-Supported Agriculture), only this is a weekly allocation of beer available to members when they stop by the brewery. Pubscribers can sign up for various levels of commitment. For $250 a year, pubscribers got a pint glass, a T-shirt, and the right to weekly refills of a 23-ounce beer mug of their own at the brewpub. For $750, they got a weekly growler refill, plus a five-gallon take-home keg refilled monthly. For $2,500 a year, the top category, the pubscriber also bought the opportunity to help make beer at the brewery.

> **tip**
>
> Make your location serve as your company calling card. Pay attention to space and place, and it will pay off in sales. No sales effort is as effective as that of the Shanty, a bar that the New York Distilling Company operates at its Brooklyn distillery, with expansive picture windows overlooking the copper stills. Drinking the product locks the sale and cements the relationship with consumers.

The campaign provided a significant cash infusion just when unexpected last-minute bills were due. With the upfront cash and a $250,000 Small Business Administration loan and their personal savings, the pair was able to finance and build their brewpub in McMinnville's downtown granary district in four months, from idea to grand opening.

"We allowed customers to take stock in the brewery themselves. To return often and feel a greater level of connectedness to the enterprise," says Kelly McDonald. "They are a part of our brewery and, in turn, we are supporting local farms by buying their hops and barley to make our beer." They've kept the interest high in their locally sourced beers through weekly music events, attended by pubscribers who receive regular MailChimp newsletters. From the start, beer sales have averaged $7,000 a week with another $18,000 in revenue from pizza and other pub food, according to McDonald.

The product must be center stage. Every shred of the marketing for Green Flash's San Diego brewery is designed to engage customers directly with their beer, says Mike Hinkley, co-owner of the brewery. With a sister brewery now under construction in Virginia Beach, Virginia, he and his wife and partner Lisa are on the road all the time. "Our whole marketing strategy is about direct interaction with customers through events like South by Southwest in Austin. We stagger entering new states, building the brand in new markets one at a time. We'll fly to a city for one beer dinner with 15 customers.

"We dedicate a lot of effort to that kind of marketing. We're small—70,000 barrels a year—and we're in 50 states. We're building the brand this way to maintain the margins. We don't discount. No time or money is spent on chain stores. We talk directly to our customers. We experience our beers with our customers, educating a core group of beer geeks and new people coming into the craft market."

"People are curious. They want to experience new things. Men bring dates who have never experienced beer in this kind of environment. With 30 sales and marketing people around the country, we set a standard and give them guidelines and sales tools, then let them be creative in how they do their jobs," says Lisa Hinkley. "Wherever we sell beer, it is at San Diego prices. We're a national specialty brand."

Having a partner like Allen Katz, head of mixology for distributor Southern Wine & Spirits, who is wired with the New York bartender network is critical, says Tom Potter, cofounder of New York Distilling Company. "We focus on 'on-premises' sales, and the cocktail culture is exploding in New York. We don't have much of a marketing budget, a couple of thousand dollars a month for everything. Hopefully we will get big enough to be able to afford more. For now we rely on free publicity and word of mouth." Media coverage, tasting events, and distillery tours are critical as well.

Craft competitions have been the critical marketing tool for Aurora, Colorado's Dry Dock Brewing (http://drydockbrewing.com). Founders Kevin DeLange and Michelle Reding launched their brewery in 2005 next door to their homebrewing store. When their Dry Dock Beer earned top medals in beer competitions that first year, word spread through online beer websites and sales soared, enabling them to expand. More awards followed, and they expanded again. "We've followed demand," says Reding. In Colorado, breweries are allowed to operate taprooms, so they could gauge consumer interest in a new beer and knew what worked immediately.

Their first brewery cost $80,000. By growing only in response to increased sales, they were able to finance

fun fact ☺

Craft competitions and festivals are big business and well worth the time and effort. After all, word-of-mouth is driven by tasting, and what better way to cultivate that buzz than to interface with your potential customers. For a full list of national beer events, visit www.craftbeer.com/news-and-events/national-events. For a full list of cider festivals, visit www.ciderguide.com/cider-festivals/. Also, see the Appendix for a detailed list of festivals.

each expansion with bank loans. Their latest expansion, in 2013, was into a new $4 million brewery capable of producing 60,000 barrels a year. From the start, their only marketing strategy was to participate in beer festivals and submit their beers to competitions, says DeLange. "We don't do a lot of other marketing because we haven't needed to do it. Winning gets you instant credibility and free advertising." After their first medals, "we were on the front page of the business section of *The Denver Post* and *The Rocky Mountain News*. And our press coverage has never stopped because we continue to win awards."

If they decide to sell beer outside of Colorado, they say they might change their marketing philosophy. But that won't happen any time soon. "We can't make enough beer to satisfy demand in Colorado at this point," says Reding. "If we go with one of the large distributors who are courting us, we'd be in a huge book with tons of other craft beer, spirits, and wine. We could get lost."

Attend any kind of festival or trade show you can, says Kent Rabish, founder of Grand Traverse Distillery (www.grandtraversedistillery.com). "When we were brand new, I would attend the bigger shows, even before we had much product. A couple of visitors who came to the booth just happened to be Costco buyers. The next thing you know, we're in five regional Costco locations in Michigan. They wanted 'craft' regional products to create a point of difference with other big chain stores.

"Our marketing budget has always been very small. If Absolut comes out with a new flavor of vodka, they support it with a $200,000 marketing push in Michigan alone. We started advertising in magazines and quickly realized it was a mistake. It was too hard to tie the expense directly to sales. Our other big mistake was paying sales reps a commission on stocking, not on sales. So for every store they put our products in, they got a fee, even when the product went into the wrong stores and just sat there collecting dust."

Distribution Means Marketing

No matter the state, at a certain point, alcoholic beverage producers who want to grow must sell their products through an independent alcoholic beverage distributor. The three-tier system—independent producers, distributors, and retailers—is a fundamental tenant of

tip

Don't discount the idea of going international. When Rabish learned American spirits are "incredibly hot overseas," he pivoted to take advantage of the demand. "And we don't have to pay a federal licensing tax when we sell outside the country," he says. "The distributor pays for all the shipping, and I get paid within 30 days. Germany and Sweden are big accounts for us."

American alcoholic beverage law. Distributors become one of the faces of a brand in their region and handle critical sales and marketing functions.

Even in states that allow self-distribution, once a brewer, distiller, or cider maker reaches a certain size, most want to stop schlepping bottles and kegs around in the back of their SUVs. If nothing else, they want someone else to take care of collecting overdue bills. Finding the right entity to handle those functions is challenging.

The relationship between producers and distributors is highly regulated in ways that sometimes make little sense. Obscure state laws may trump what is written in a duly signed contract. This is a relationship that must be discussed with a legal advisor well versed in alcoholic beverage distribution. All proposed contracts need to be reviewed by legal counsel. With laws varying state-by-state, frequently distributors are as unaware of them as the novice producer. Regardless, significant damage can be done that can haunt businesses for years.

Know your options. Meet with as many of the distributors in your region as you can and learn their sales philosophy. Does it match up with yours? Who else do they represent? Ask those producers if they are happy with the distributor's efforts. Would they change, if they could? To which other distributor? Why? You are hiring the distributor to be part of your team. Be sure you trust them with the future of your company.

Frustrated with its lack of a good distribution option, Brooklyn Brewery created its own distribution company in the 1990s, operating it separately from the brewery. "We sold our distribution company for $12 million in 2004," says cofounder Steve Hindy. "Big distributors are eager to represent craft now. We no longer go to them on bended knee. Now they come to us." It is still a fraught relationship. Distributors are dealing with more brands, more products than they may be equipped to handle. "The coming shakeout in craft beer," says Hindy, "may well come down to who gets good distribution and who doesn't."

Stone Brewing Company also built its own separate distribution company. "We had no other choice but to become distributors. No wholesaler would distribute our beer. It was extremely financially burdensome to build it," says Stone Brewing cofounder Greg Koch. "Then after a year and a half, we turned the corner on it and it became viable." Launched in 1996, Stone Distributing now represents 35 craft brands throughout a 40,000-square-mile footprint in Southern California with a population of 20 million. Industry analysts estimate Stone's distributing company would be worth $100 million if they sold it today. "We know how to take care of beer. We have the largest refrigerated fleet in Southern California, perhaps the country."

"A distributor who passed on us gave me a pat on the head and told me we were going nowhere. Well, that distributor is out of business today, and we're doing just fine. Access to the market has always been challenging for craft. It's just that the character of the challenge has changed. It used to be they didn't understand our beers. Now there is lots of interest in our beers, but it is an extremely crowded market and consumers have a lot of choices," says Koch. The friction is on the store shelf and in the bar taps.

"As craft beer emerged in the 1990s, the little distributors took the craft beers no one else wanted," says Dennis Hartman, head of the craft beer and spirits division at California distributor Wine Warehouse. "It was hard at first. Wine Warehouse never had any of the big beers; we were always the alternative network. As craft grew, it was our whole portfolio. It wasn't easy but we were poised for what is happening now. We have 40 to 50 American craft beers, 35 Germans, 60 Belgians. Our book is really big.

aha!

"The best marketing for craft is to open your doors. Big beer companies market their crafty beers with obfuscation and sleight of hand. Truth and justice are on our side," says Greg Koch, cofounder of Stone Brewing.

"Artisan spirits is the fastest-growing sector of our business," Hartman says. "Up-and-coming brands don't want to sit behind the big brands. To get a foothold in the market, they must be hand sold. You have to tell their story. They make these things, but they don't have a marketing budget to support them. We do it for them. Now we have what everyone is looking for. We're a major player in craft." See Figure 8–1 for a list of other big players and Figure 8–2 for the top states in which they play, both on page 131.

New craft brands are entering a "rotation heavy market," according to distributors. There are more brands than shelf space, so retailers constantly shuffle their offerings. The best distributors know their craft clients inside and out, and share that knowledge with the community. They work directly with restaurant chefs and bartenders to develop pairings featuring craft products. They organize tap takeovers at local bars and restaurants where host locations put a brewer's most popular beers on tap for a night, and customers get to taste great beer and learn all about a particular brand. These events are most successful when the distributor has educated the bar staff and is at the event to answer customer questions. Pouring samples at beer and food festivals as well as music and sporting events is a constant effort.

Terry Cekola is the founder of Colorado distributor Elite Brands, a specialist in craft beer, spirits, and wine. "In Colorado, we have a great law that brewers can self-distribute. It's fabulous; we totally support it. It's best for them financially in the beginning. They can save a lot of money. They get reaction directly from the marketplace, the customers, about what works and what doesn't. So when we meet with them, hopefully their beer is priced correctly.

Top 15 BA Craft Brands Based on Dollar Sales
Total U.S. - Supermarkets

Samuel Adams Rebel IPA is already a Top 10 BA Craft Brand based on Dollar Sales YTD

	Dollar Sales		Dollar Share of Craft	
	YTD	% Chg YA	YTD	Chg YA
SIERRA NEVADA PALE ALE (1)	$32,949,134	3.5%	4.5%	-0.7%
SAMUEL ADAMS SEASONAL (2)	$32,688,041	23.4%	4.5%	0.1%
SAMUEL ADAMS BOSTON LAGER (3)	$27,070,646	6.4%	3.7%	-0.5%
NEW BELGIUM FAT TIRE AMBER ALE (4)	$23,522,835	25.6%	3.2%	0.1%
SIERRA NEVADA TORPEDO EXTRA IPA (5)	$16,408,884	7.5%	2.3%	-0.3%
SAMUEL ADAMS VARIETY PACK (6)	$16,068,277	-12.4%	2.2%	-0.8%
SHINER BOCK (7)	$15,673,558	8.3%	2.2%	-0.2%
LAGUNITAS INDIA PALE ALE (8)	$13,480,385	70.9%	1.9%	0.5%
SAMUEL ADAMS REBEL IPA (9)	$10,218,768		1.4%	1.4%
NEW BELGIUM RANGER IPA (10)	$9,728,767	30.9%	1.3%	0.1%
SIERRA NEVADA SEASONAL (11)	$9,370,608	-6.3%	1.3%	-0.4%
NEW BELGIUM VARIETY PACK (12)	$8,594,734	70.7%	1.2%	0.3%
BELLS SEASONAL (13)	$7,574,778	22.0%	1.0%	0.0%
NEW BELGIUM SEASONAL (14)	$7,405,039	37.8%	1.0%	0.1%
STONE INDIA PALE ALE (15)	$5,579,549	17.7%	0.8%	0.0%

IRI Data : YTD 2014 Ending 07.13.14

IRI

Copyright © 2014 Information Resources, Inc. (IRI) Confidential and Proprietary.   38

FIGURE 8–1: **List of Top 15 Craft Beer Brands by Dollar Sales**
Credit: IRI PowerPoint Slide #38.

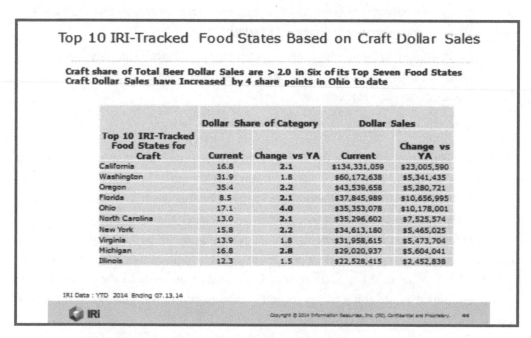

Top 10 IRI-Tracked Food States Based on Craft Dollar Sales

Craft share of Total Beer Dollar Sales are > 2.0 in Six of its Top Seven Food States
Craft Dollar Sales have Increased by 4 share points in Ohio to date

Top 10 IRI-Tracked Food States for Craft	Dollar Share of Category		Dollar Sales	
	Current	Change vs YA	Current	Change vs YA
California	16.8	2.1	$134,331,059	$23,005,590
Washington	31.9	1.8	$60,172,638	$5,341,435
Oregon	35.4	2.2	$43,539,658	$5,280,721
Florida	8.5	2.1	$37,845,989	$10,656,995
Ohio	17.1	4.0	$35,353,078	$10,178,001
North Carolina	13.0	2.1	$35,296,602	$7,525,574
New York	15.8	2.2	$34,613,180	$5,465,025
Virginia	13.9	1.8	$31,958,615	$5,473,704
Michigan	16.8	2.8	$29,020,937	$5,604,041
Illinois	12.3	1.5	$22,528,415	$2,452,838

IRI Data : YTD 2014 Ending 07.13.14

IRI

Copyright © 2014 Information Resources, Inc. (IRI) Confidential and Proprietary.   44

FIGURE 8–2: **List of Top Ten States for Craft Beer Sales**
Credit: IRI PowerPoint Slide #44.

▶ Taking Stock with New Clients

Cekola's team runs through a checklist with new clients to make certain they have thought through all the important distribution issues.

- ▶ *Do they have enough kegs?* A brewery needs four or five to support one bar tap.

- ▶ *Do they have the right packaging for their beer style?* A strong beer can be in a four-bottle pack. Lighter beers are best in six-packs.

- ▶ *What about cans?* The mobile canning companies launched four years ago that drive to breweries are now widely available, making canning affordable for small breweries.

- ▶ *Do they date their beers?* Craft beer is a fresh product that is rarely pasteurized. It goes stale quickly. "Freshness" dates stamped on the bottles are popular and smart selling tools. It is important to remember that the popularity of craft beer fell in the 1990s, in part, because many breweries did not have systems to remove stale beer from stores.

- ▶ *Are they up on the style trends?* IPAs have been hot for a while, and they are not going away. Seasonal beers—small production, allocated beers—have always been incredibly popular. But the hottest trend today is session beers, lower-alcohol beers that are easy to drink. Craft brewers never call them light beers—while session beers are lower alcohol, they are not necessarily lower calorie—but they are more approachable than the higher-alcohol, complex beers craft is famous for making.

- ▶ *Do they have a local following?* The rise of the local neighborhood brewery is good for craft. Certain beers are only available in their hometowns. The next town has its specialty beer. Close-to-home beer sells best.

"Quality is the main thing we talk about. That's more important than what vessel you put it in or what flavor it is. And be a good community member. What is so special about the craft industry is that it's so collaborative. They live by the idea that a rising tide lifts all boats. People who are successful in this business are the ones who help each other.

"We talk with them about financing. You aren't just going to pop in a new brewhouse and go to work the next day. When we get serious about bringing a new brewery in, they've been up and running a while," Cekola says. They need to understand their potential for growth and how they are going to pay for it. Distributors don't want clients to run out of beer.

Shovels at
the Gold Rush

Selling equipment for the craft business is *big* business. With so many small breweries, distilleries, and cideries opening, the people supplying these producers are working overtime to meet demand. And their businesses are thriving. "In Portland, we're seeing new brewery equipment fabricators," says Kurt Widmer, founder of Widmer Brothers Brewery, a unit of Craft Brew

Alliance. "There was one and now there are five and all are doing very well. There are now four universities in Washington and Oregon with brewery programs. The industry has created 8,000 jobs in Oregon alone. Barriers to entry are low, and failure rate is even lower."

Is the Equipment Niche for You?

Robert Soltys and his wife, Michelle, owners of Premiere Stainless Systems in Escondido, California, are among the few American manufacturing business owners whose fortunes took off as the recession was looming. Ever since, they've been racing to keep up with demand for the brewhouses they fabricate. "We have had the same pricing for three years; we are so busy, we haven't had time to look at raising them. Customers are willing to pay more to get their systems faster, but we can't make them faster," says Michelle Soltys.

"We've gone from two employees five years ago to 30 employees today," she says. In 2012, they sold 50 brew systems; in 2014, they sold twice as many, with customers in Australia, New Zealand, Argentina, Kenya, Spain, and Israel.

"We started in 2000 with the idea that we just wanted to be part of the beer industry. Five years from now I think we will be just as stressed. I don't see it slowing down. Everyone who orders a system is back in three months ordering more tanks so they can expand," says Soltys.

Selling brewery equipment is the equivalent of having the shovel concession at the gold rush. Everyone in the business is working as hard and as fast as they can to meet the demand for new or bigger breweries. Look for equipment, supplies, and services new breweries, distilleries, and cideries need, and ask yourself if these are business opportunities for you. Few craft producers have experience with advertising, a piece of the marketing puzzle that will be more important going forward. A quick look at craft websites is all you need to see the crying need for both web and graphic designers. Small technological enhancements to brewhouses and stills sell quickly by word-of-mouth across this well-connected industry.

>
>
> **tip**
>
> Don't be held back by your geographic location. Thanks to the online market, some of your best customers can come from other continents.

The Growing Equipment Market

In 2009, the typical new brewery was a three-barrel system, which means that the maximum size of each batch of beer was three barrels, says Soltys. It went to five to seven barrels a couple of years ago. Now 15- or 30-barrel systems are the norm. "They have figured out they have to go as big as they can afford to go right out of the gate. A brewer's biggest challenge is keeping up with demand. If you start small, you will have to change out your system in a year." At Premiere Stainless Systems, the standard 15-barrel microbrew system is around $210,000. It costs around $340,000 for a 30-barrel system. "We've seen the ups and downs, weathered the 1990s nosedive and the slow early 2000s. Then when everyone around us was losing their jobs, the market for breweries took off. I guess beer is an affordable luxury because people were sure drinking it when the economy tanked." There are 90 breweries in San Diego now and another 60 planning to open. And guess what? All of them need someone to sell and service their equipment needs.

Business Is Hopping

The market for hops, the green herb used in all traditional beer recipes, has been on a boom/bust cycle for decades. Originally, craft brewers bought hops on the spot, picking up whatever the big beer companies didn't buy. But hops are expensive to grow. And when craft took off, hops farmers hadn't anticipated the demand. There wasn't enough to go around. Today, craft producers sign five-year contracts for the hops they want, giving hops farmers the ability to plan ahead.

> **fun fact** ☺
>
> Hop ratio is much higher in craft beers, says Ann George. Big Beer only uses a quarter of a pound of hops for every barrel of beer (31 gallons). Craft uses an average of 1.3 pounds of hops in an average barrel of their beer.

"Thanks to the craft industry, a five-year forward contract is now the industry standard," says Ann George, executive director of the nonprofit, Hop Growers of America. As a result, the hops industry has been profitable for the last three to five years. "Craft has turned our industry around. They have set very high expectations for quality. They want more and better varieties, and they are funding the research to support that. The growers who have stepped up are benefiting from the boom. We now have on-farm cold storage, cleaner facilities, and a wider range of quality indicators than Big Brewers ever considered important. And craft is willing to pay us enough to maintain these improvements."

There now are hops growers in 14 new states, and an additional 880 acres of hops has been planted. There are 180 growers farming 150 acres of hops in New York State alone. "Hops has terroir," says George. "The different hop varieties taste different when grown in different places. Yakima hops taste different from those grown in Michigan. It's like wine grapes. Thanks to craft, we are in a new discovery period for hops."

Supply Side Economics

"It is fair to say we are selling shovels at the gold rush," says Jake Keeler, director of marketing at Brewing Supply Group (BSG), a supplier working across all craft alcoholic beverage sectors. BSG has seen sales grow between 15 percent and 20 percent every year, in both dollars and volume, for several years. "We're seeing a lot of money flowing into craft. There is talk of a bubble, but we can see that the growth is real. There still are places in the country that are underserved. Opportunities are greatest in the Southwest and Southeast and the Great Plains states. All are underserved. This industry is going to continue to grow at this rate. In 2016, it might begin to slow down, but it won't fall off.

"We talk about the failure rate for breweries every day. It is crazy: maybe 7 percent. This is an unprecedented industry," says Keeler. "The new breweries are opening with more capacity than they did even a few years ago. They start with a multistate distribution plan and a 30-barrel system, which used to be the size of the second expansion. Or, they open really small, no investors, a five-year plan to serve just a four- or five-mile radius, that's what I recommend. They build their markets organically. No marketing budget. Self-distribute. By the time they go to investors they are debt-free and making a profit. They live within their means and survive, like a local baker who lives above his store."

Making the Jump to a New Product

The craft business is easy to transition within, and for good reason. Many of the methods, business planning functions, and marketing translate well from one type of brewing or distilling to another. For example, "Distilling has the capacity to be like craft brewing, only the product sells for much more, and the craft producers don't seem to be much of a threat to the big distillers," says Keeler. There are new distilleries opening all the time. It's all tied to the demand for locally produced and sourced products. The transition from being a craft beer drinker to being a craft spirits and hard cider drinker is easy to make. That person is already into experimenting.

Another wide-open niche is the used equipment market, which is ridiculous (in a good way), says ProBrewer.com owner Tom McCormick, who also runs the California Brewers Association. ProBrewer is the only source for classified ads for used brewery equipment. "Now that the lead time on new equipment is 6 to 12 months or more, the advantage to buying used is that is

> ### fun fact ☺
> Distilling may be the cheaper choice in terms of startup cost. The equipment for distilling compared to brewing is relatively inexpensive. Raw ingredients are less, and you don't need many ingredients. You can make a white spirit in 14 days and sell it immediately.

it available immediately. But used equipment costs about the same as new equipment. The more moving parts to the item, the higher the potential wear and tear and the lower the cost when it is used.

"Used equipment gets snatched up very, very quickly. If you start a small brewery, when it is time to grow, you are able to sell your equipment for what you paid for it," McCormick says. Right now, the most popular approach is to start with a seven-barrel system with a tasting room and sell as much beer as you can through that tasting room, then self-distribute the rest through kegs or bottles. When it is time to expand, sell the equipment that doesn't work in the larger system to help finance the growth.

Clearly, it's boom time for craft across the board, even as the country recovers from a down economy. So what's holding you back? Go west, young man or woman. The gold rush awaits.

Defining Craft in a New Era

Despite their popularity, the craft alcoholic beverage sectors are struggling with an identity crisis that threatens their continued robust growth rate. Like the faddish buzzwords "natural" and "healthy," the definition of "craft" can have little to do with the image it evokes. The sector has grown far beyond its original reference to small, hands-on, independent producers making goods on a nonindustrial scale. How about "artisan"? Is this a better word? Neither descriptor has a legally enforceable definition. Any beer, spirits, or cider maker can use either term, and as the popularity of these sectors grows, the rampant misuse increases.

Confusion creates opportunities to appear to be one thing when you are really something else. Invariably, such choices are made to enhance sales. It is easy to make the wrong choice.

"There is a lot of argument about defining craft. You can't put a size on it, or you punish someone for being successful. Continuous, automated distilling is pretty industrial," says Cris Steller, head of the California Artisan Distillery Guild and cofounder of Dry Diggings Distillery. "If you buy that industrial alcohol then treat it by just cutting it with water, filtering it, that's not much craft." But there are plenty of "craft" distilleries that do little more.

tip

The best "craft" marketing is educating consumers so they can discern when they are paying a premium for superior quality with distinctive individuality. There may be no controlling the use of the term "craft," but transparency is a distinction that illustrates the difference.

The language that carries meaning in craft sectors is the language of story, the story of how the product is made and who made it. The more detailed and verifiable the story, the more likely it is truthful. When consumers are presented with solid information, they trust it. Increasingly, craft guilds are calling for members to distinguish themselves with transparency and encourage site tours that put their processes on display.

"I'm sure you are aware of what has been happening for the last six months," says David Perkins, founder and owner of High West Distillery in Park City, Utah. Anyone interested in spirits would understand the reference. It started with the publication of *The Kings County Distillery Guide to Urban Moonshining: How to Make and Drink Whiskey*, by Colin Spoelman and David Haskell at the end of 2013, a superb book that anyone who enjoys spirits should read. The authors took the time and effort to explain how whiskey is made in the U.S. It was a bombshell of revelations and a public relations disaster for the craft spirits sector.

The controversial story was about a particular stash of rye whiskey produced at a Lawrenceburg, Indiana, industrial distillery once owned by Seagram's and now a division of Midwest Grain Products (MGP). The rye whiskey in this story is 95 percent rye, compared to the typical 70 percent rye whiskeys. It was developed by Seagram's to be blended into Seagram's 7. When the company sold off its spirits business in the 1990s to finance a disastrous foray into Hollywood, this high rye whiskey was sold on the wholesale market. "This rye was considered rot gut," says Arthur Shapiro, former head of marketing for Seagrams. "It was inexpensive and easy to produce with caramel coloring added to make it appear more appealing." The high rye content made it particularly spicy, which worked in the Seagram's 7 blend but was never expected to stand on its own.

High West Distillery

That rye, with the extra barrel aging afforded by abandonment, eventually became the juice peddled by many "craft" spirits brands as their own distillate—Templeton Rye, Redemption Rye, Bulleit Rye, Willet, Smooth Ambler, and George Dickel Rye, among others. Spoelman and Haskell's diagram of the "American Whiskey Family Tree" showing the origins of various whiskeys has been reproduced and hangs on the wall of craft distilleries eager to show they are *not* on the chart. High West (www.highwest.com), however, is on the chart.

The New York Times and Atlantic magazine wrote stories and even CBS Evening News took a shot at the idea that there is less "craft" in the craft spirits sector than most consumers think. Perkins and his team at High West, however, emerged with their reputation intact. While the High West labels may have lacked transparency, the company didn't make false claims about their product.

Perkins moved to Park City in 2004, after a career in biopharmaceuticals in the San Francisco Bay area, hoping to start a hobby career as a distiller. He eventually built what seemed like a good-size copper still that could produce 10,000-proof gallons of spirits a year inside a ski-in/ski-out distillery/restaurant near the town's chairlift. The prime real estate set him back $6 million, but it was a good investment. "Half our revenue comes from our restaurant in that building, which we didn't see coming when we opened," Perkins says.

"Distilling is a capital-intensive business," he says. "It's expensive. You have to be clever." In 2007, High West became Utah's first licensed distillery since Prohibition, with the restaurant opening a year later. He had aged whiskey ready to sell when High West opened its doors.

The trick was the Seagram's rye. A friend at Kentucky's Four Roses Distillery (http://kybourbontrail.com) shared the secret to starting a new brand of whiskey: Buy someone else's until your own is ready to sell. "I went to the Indiana plant and tried this rye that no one had ever bottled on its own," says Perkins. He bought everything he could afford, $300,000 worth of aged rye, "which was a whole lot of money for us then." Perkins was the first in a long line of craft distillers to buy that Indiana rye. "It exploded after we bought it," says Perkins, sparking a rye renaissance that continues today.

High West's first product was Rendezvous Rye, a blend of the Seagram's spirits and a 16-year-old rye produced at the Barton Distillery in Kentucky. "We didn't want to sell the Indiana rye alone. Anyone can do that. Blending took it to a new level. This gave us the luxury of time to perfect what we were doing in the distillery." Those early years were full of failed efforts. "We had to dump a lot of bad stuff down the drain. There are 50 places to screw up when you go from grain to glass."

Ten years into his second career as a distiller, Perkins is selling High West in 44 states and has some of his own aged whiskey in the mix, he says. With a new 30,000-square-foot distillery capable of producing 700,000-proof gallons opening east of Park City next to a boutique hotel, he will be making a lot more of it. "It takes a lot of money to run four 500-gallon stills," says Perkins. "Buying spirits and blending them got us to this point. We still buy from the Seagram's old plant. We buy a lot of what they've already distilled and a little bit of what we ask them to do for us. We've learned how good the big guys are at what they do.

"Would I do anything any differently? No. I'm pretty happy. Blending existing whiskeys is paramount to our success," he says. "No one likes to be duped. We were selling a 10-year-old whiskey when we hadn't been open that long. It was hard to *not* tell the truth in that circumstance." Today, about 20 percent of High West's spirits are produced in its own stills.

High West was always upfront about what they were doing," says Nicole Austin, King's County Distillery's master blender. "Buying spirits is a shortcut. It's a way to build a brand while you wait for your spirits to age. A lot of people bought [aged industrial spirits] cheap and sold them high," says Austin. "There is a long history of market fluffery with whiskey. But we are coming to a sea change. Consumers are not going to accept it anymore," she says.

"The difference is telling your story without guile. Almost every craft product is in the premium category, even if by cost alone. But there are plenty of noncraft producers selling their whiskey at craft prices." Consumers want to know they are paying for something special. "The heart and soul of the spirits industry is up for grabs. It is hard not to feel rage when someone tells a bullshit story. The goal of craft is to expand what spirits can be, not to copy what is already out there," says Austin. "I hope we come out on the one-for-all side. No one wants to be lectured to when they drink."

The definition of "craft" with distillers is "extremely frustrating," says Paul Hletko, founder of Few Spirits (www.fewspirits.com) in Chicago. "I know what it takes to do this, and it would be a lot easier to just buy the stuff. My costs per bottle would go from $9 to about 50 cents." Still, Hletko believes there is room under the craft umbrella for anyone who discloses how they produce their spirits. "Consumers should simply be told the truth up front. Once you think someone is lying to you, you think everyone is. It hurts all the other small distillers."

Hletko started Few Spirits in 2008 and has had his spirits available on the market for three years. "Our sales are tiny. We work really hard. It looks romantic from the outside, and we do it because we love it. But it's a surprise to a lot of people how difficult it is to introduce a packaged good to the consumer market. A lot of people right now are just holding on. The opportunity is less than what people think it is. Don't do it if you have less than $20 million."

Tito's Handmade Vodka

To the distillers who are truly crafting their spirits from grain to glass, Bert "Tito" Beveridge is an irritating pebble in their shoe. He launched Tito's Handmade Vodka (www.titosvodka. com) in 1997 in Austin, Texas, and now produces an estimated 10 million cases of what is little more than industrially produced neutral grain spirits that he cuts with water and appears to pass through only one last distillation process.

The American Craft Spirits Association, where Beveridge is a member, "is heavily engaged in the discussion of truth in advertising," says Ralph Erenzo. "We have ethics agreements members must sign. It has to do with transparency, saying whether you actually distilled it. One of the problems is that the law is ambiguous on this point." And Beveridge's membership in the association is a contentious topic. No one but Tito seems to believe there is anything "handmade" about his vodka. "We want penalties on the producers of untruthful labels," says Erenzo. "It is important for the whole industry. Too many people buy their spirits and then put their own label on it." The problem with Tito's and Templeton Rye is "the labels imply they made it," he says.

In the beer sector, the equivalent controversy has been over contract brewing, where a craft brewer gives a recipe to a larger brewery and pays it to have that beer produced and bottled. Contract brewing is still frowned upon by most craft brewers, but the practice is increasingly rare, reducing its divisiveness. No one begrudges the success of the big craft brewers, who have all grown while producing consistently high-quality beers made with traditional ingredients. And while not all craft beer is well made, there seems to be no one who substitutes cheap corn in a mash they claim is barley malt.

fun fact

"Neutral grain spirits (NGS) cost 60 cents a gallon," says Ralph Erenzo, noting that Tito's Vodka makes 10 million cases a year using NGS, making a fortune selling a slightly cheaper "premium" vodka.

The identity questions focus on distribution and marketing. Is 10 Barrel still a craft brewery if it is owned by Anheuser-Busch? Most craft brewers say it is not. While their product has not changed, the muscle behind it certainly has. The Brewers Association has thrown them out of the craft club, just as it did Craft Brew Alliance, Goose Island, Blue Point, and other small breweries purchased whole or more than 25 percent by larger breweries. Breweries with major stakes held by nonbeer industry investors, however, remain welcome . . . for now. The debate continues and the ownership issue will only heat up as more founders retire and look for ways to cash out of their companies.

As for cider, it is defined as either "artisan" or "industrial" and is rarely referred to as "craft." Artisan ciders are pure fruit juice—predominately apples but also pears, quince, and other pomme fruits. Most rely on added yeast, and sometimes an added fresh fruit juice, such as elderberry, for a distinctive flavor. The difference between these beverages and their industrial brethren can be read on the side of the bottle. Reconstituted apple juice and high fructose corn syrup are industrial ingredients. Still, it is not a battle royal over identity similar to what is happening in craft spirits.

One of the best ways to hammer out these issues of identity is to consider what makes your craft product unique and special, what sets it apart from other beverages in the craft market. To do that, you need a "unique selling proposition."

Understanding Your Unique Selling Proposition

Before you can begin to sell your product to anyone else, you have to sell yourself on it. This is especially important when your product or service is similar to those around you. Very few businesses are one of a kind. Just look around you: How many clothing retailers, hardware stores, air conditioning installers, and electricians are truly unique? Likewise, how many craft brewers are truly unique?

The key to effective selling in this situation is what advertising and marketing professionals call a unique selling proposition (USP). Unless you can pinpoint what makes your business unique in a world of homogeneous competitors, you cannot target your sales efforts successfully.

Pinpointing your USP requires some hard soul-searching and creativity. One way to start is to analyze how other companies use their USPs to their advantage. This requires careful analysis of other companies' ads and marketing messages. If you analyze what they say they sell, not just their product or service characteristics, you can learn a great deal about how companies distinguish themselves from competitors.

Each of these is an example of a company that has found a USP "peg" on which to hang its marketing strategy. A business can peg its USP on product characteristics, price structure, placement strategy (location and distribution), or promotional strategy. These are what marketers call the "four P's" of marketing. They are used to give a business a market position that sets it apart from the competition.

Here's how to uncover your USP and use it to power up your sales:

▶ *Put yourself in your customer's shoes.* Too often, entrepreneurs fall in love with their product or service and forget that it is the customer's needs, not their own, that they must satisfy. Step back from your daily operations and carefully scrutinize what your customers really want. Suppose you own a brewpub. Sure, customers come into your location for beer. But is beer all they want? What could make them come back again and again and ignore your competition? The answer might be quality, convenience, reliability, friendliness, cleanliness, courtesy, or customer service.

Remember, price is never the only reason people buy. If your competition is beating you on pricing because they are larger, you have to find another sales feature that addresses the customer's needs and then build your sales and promotional efforts around that feature.

▶ *Uncover the real reasons customers buy your product instead of a competitor's.* As your business grows, you'll be able to ask your best source of information: your customers. You will be surprised how honest people are when you ask how you can improve your service.

▶ *Since your business is just starting out, you won't have a lot of customers to ask yet, so ask your competition instead.* Craft producers routinely drop into each other's breweries, distilleries, and cider houses to see what's happening and talk with their competitors. It's part of the craft ethos of openness and mutual support. You can see firsthand how customers respond to products and chat with them about their preferences.

Once you have thought through your unique selling proposition, you need to take the next—and hardest—step: clearing your mind of any preconceived ideas about your product or service and be brutally honest with yourself. What features of your business jump out at you as something that sets you apart? What can you promote that will make customers want to patronize your business? How can you position your business to highlight your USP? Do not get discouraged. Successful business ownership is not about having a unique product or service; it's about making your product stand out—even in a market filled with similar items.

When you choose a type of craft beverage industry with which to align yourself, considering these identity politics first is a smart move. Know your product, know its market, and be sure you are able to create a clearly defined brand that does not rely solely on the latest perception of the product, nor on a contrived marketing ploy. Work with pure product, practice truth in advertising, and work hard to ensure that your brand identity is clear to the consumer.

Does the Party End?

The beauty of craft has been that you can start out small and learn as you grow. That has never been truer than it is today. The growth, however, used to come as a result of backbreaking work. Today, growth can happen far more quickly and with less effort. It can be a function of being located in the right place. It can come from a fat check from an investor. Or you can be successful in a niche that makes you attractive to a larger company that needs to diversify.

The free-for-all will become more chaotic with so many early craft founders looking to retire, move on, or step back, and so many large industrial beverage companies seeking to buy in, takeover, or dominate. Change will happen quickly with unexpected ramifications.

"Every brewery you can name is ripe for being bought out. But they won't do it. They'll be seen as sellouts by other craft breweries. It would tarnish their image," says Michael Lewis, professor emeritus of Brewing Science at University of California, Davis.

"The next younger generation might sell," Lewis says. "They make superb beer, but aren't quite making it financially and can't afford to expand. They are successful, but struggling in the middle, making 100,000 to 150,000 barrels a year. They can make a deal that allows them to continue to be engaged in their breweries." These companies—new players entering the craft industry that are neither the independent-minded entrepreneurs who founded craft, nor the giant industrial companies like Anheuser-Busch that craft has worked to defeat—are a mystery. No one knows who these new players will be or what effect they will have on craft.

The disruptive effect of the big companies playing in craft's small sandbox may not end to their advantage. Craft is interchangeable to the vast majority of consumers, regardless of who owns the brand. Once consumers develop a taste for craft, they stick with the higher quality, more flavorful beverage. They don't go back to the cheap stuff.

Rather than blunting crafts' most powerful marketing tool—the ability to differentiate themselves from industrial producers—the involvement of Anheuser-Busch and MillerCoors in craft helps grow the craft sector at the expense of Budweiser and Coors, says Beer Market Insight's Steinman. With Blue Moon (MillerCoors) and Shock Top (Anheuser-Busch), "they invited drinkers to switch to craft," says Steinman, and it is speeding the erosion of sales for their flagship brands.

Price is the wild card with craft. Bigger companies with efficiencies of scale can start price wars that craft producers cannot win. In fact, they cannot even play. Gaining market share by cutting prices is such a dangerous game for craft producers, it has happened

tip

Stay loyal to craft and protect your identity. "Craft breweries aren't growing the beer market. They are taking market share away from big beer companies, and those companies are going to buy anything they can to gain craft legitimacy. But only an idiot would think you could quickly build a craft beer brand with the idea that you can sell it to Big Beer," says Lewis.

only on rare occasions. Anheuser-Busch and MillerCoors have the advantage here. They could drop the price of their "craft-ish" or craft satellite brands and leave it there for as long as it takes to squeeze the craft competition. But with revenues tanking, there are just as many reasons to believe that Big Beer will avoid doing anything that depresses craft prices. In fact, it may turn out that craft creates a rising tide that truly does lift all boats, even the big companies, as consumers become used to paying a premium for higher quality food and beverages.

Craft isn't a fad or a trend. It is part of major shift in how consumers view what they eat and drink. And, so far, the transition to new owners has been quite civilized. Everyone appears to be concerned with the long-term viability of these companies as well as the craft sector.

There are many ways to cash out of a company. But many craft producers, particularly the pioneers of the American craft beer and spirits movement are people with an anti-industrial, anti-corporate streak. When there is news of a craft company being purchased by Anheuser-Busch, other craft producers respond as if a friend has died. Someone they know "went to the dark side." That is what John McDonald and Fritz Maytag faced when they were ready to retire.

This limited their options for selling their companies and moving on to other things, or even simply retiring. Below are the stories of these two craft pioneers. They sold their companies and are happy they did. And they did it in such a way that the rest of their craft sector is applauding their moves. The stories offer insights into the craft culture and the type of people who have led the industry, but also the difficulty of passing the torch from one generation to the next. It took these founders years to find the people they trusted with the future of their companies. As more of the first generation of craft producers seeks to retire, this transition may grow easier. There will certainly be more and more options with so many new people wanting into the craft sector. The largest craft companies will grow larger, and there will be more opportunities to work for them and gain the training you need to start your own venture.

These succession stories are still unfolding. They've started well and it will be illustrative to see how these companies fare over the coming years.

Anchor Brewing and Anchor Distilling

It was a whim acted on quickly with little thought. That's how Fritz Maytag often speaks of his decision in 1965 to buy Anchor Brewing (www.anchorbrewing.com). That whim turned into a passion that lasted 45 years. By the time he was ready to sell the company, Maytag moved far more slowly. Anchor was both a craft brewery and a craft distillery as well as the sum of his life's work.

Maytag spent years meeting with potential new owners, but no one felt like the right fit. Then six years after he first met with Keith Greggor and Tony Foglio, he circled back to them to shake hands with the guys who were shepherding Skyy Vodka through an explosive growth phase that culminated with the sale of the brand to liquor giant Gruppo Campari. It doesn't get less craft than that. The father of the American craft beer and spirits movement sold his baby to a couple of Big Booze hacks.

At least that's how it looked to some people in the industry at the time. Four years later, it is clear Maytag saw something in the pair that may not have been obvious to others. Anchor is growing at a much faster pace, certainly, but it has not lost its focus on innovation, creativity, or quality. Decisions are made with a respect for the authenticity of the Anchor brand, says David King, head of the distillery. No one cuts corners.

"Fritz was a very careful seller with interesting requirements," says Greggor. Out of respect for the historical significance of the Potrero Hill brewery in San Francisco, he wanted the brewery and distillery to stay where they were, and he wanted his employees to stay there, too. "These are things that are difficult to put into contracts. So it came down to faith," Greggor says. Partnered with Berry Brothers & Rudd, a 300-year-old London wine and spirits merchant for the Anchor deal, the pair also owned San Diego-based Preiss Imports, which had a portfolio of craft spirits brands from around the world. Greggor and Foglio also had invested in BrewDog, a sensational British craft brewery.

"Berry Brothers is a huge believer in education with their wines," says Greggor. "And that's the way to approach craft consumers as well. Developing the Anchor brands would be about education." They folded Preiss Imports into Anchor Distilling (www. anchordistilling.com). But they kept operations, sales, and distribution of Anchor's beers separate from Anchor's spirits, which required doubling their sales staff from 12 to 25. "It was a grand experiment. No one had ever done anything like this before. It was a scary time," says Greggor. "People drive this business. It is always about the people. We tripled the spirits business in four years." Anchor Brewing's beer sales have doubled, and the company announced plans to build a second brewery near the Giants baseball stadium that will add 500,000 barrels to Anchor's overall production capacity, which is currently close to 200,000 barrels at the historic Potrero Hill plant.

"The category is vibrant," says Greggor. "A lot of private equity money is floating around. But you cannot build your business fast enough to satisfy those people. The last thing we want is venture capital money. The new brewery ensures our survival" as independent craft producers.

"The credit for Anchor's successful transition goes to Fritz," says David King, who runs the distillery. "He laid the foundation we are building on. Fritz would recognize everything we are doing; we've just increased the pace a bit, put more resources behind the ideas." Craft spirits is about telling a story. Every one of our products has a story that is true to Anchor and San Francisco," he says.

Boulevard Brewery

In the fall of 2013, John McDonald sold his Kansas City-based Boulevard Brewing Company (www.boulevard.com) to the Duvel Moortgat Brewery, a fourth-generation, family-owned Belgian beer company, for $125 to $150 million, according to industry analysts. The 12th largest U.S. craft brewer at the time, Boulevard produced 185,000 barrels of beer that year. Duvel is smaller than some U.S. craft breweries, making 700,000 barrels. Speaking to a Brewbound conference, McDonald said he started thinking about selling the brewery when he turned 59.

"We needed to take Boulevard to the next level," says McDonald. "We needed a lot of things. And I had become disengaged. I was part of the problem. Selling the brewery was part of solving that problem. It was very emotional. In my mind, I did the right thing. I impulsively got into the beer business, and I impulsively got out."

McDonald said he considered selling the company to his staff in an ESOP—an employee stock option plan—a frequently discussed endgame for craft brewery pioneers. January of that year, New Belgium Brewing Company founder Kim Jordan had sold all of her family's interest and control of the brewery to employees through a long-established ESOP already holding a 41 percent interest in America's third-largest craft brewer. Deschutes Brewery, Full Sail Brewing, and Alaskan Brewing have taken advantage of the succession tool's advantageous tax provisions and established ESOPs holding minority interests in their breweries. And as of August 2014, an ESOP formed by Boston's Harpoon Brewery holds 48 percent of the company, allowing cofounder Rich Doyle and other early investors to liquidate some of their holdings.

Private equity offers were considered and rejected, says McDonald, noting that the brewery would have been in flux until those investors flipped it to other owners. "It would go someplace I didn't intend for it to go."

Discussions of a sale to MillerCoors became serious, McDonald says. "It didn't seem right to me. They're good guys, but wasn't the right fit. Once we started talking with Duvel, the more I looked at it—and they are one of my favorite beers—it seemed right. Duvel kind of invented craft beer. They've been selling high-margin beer longer than any of us."

McDonalds' lawyers advised him to step out of the negotiation and let them handle it, which was fine by the then 60-year-old brewer. But when the negotiations started to stall and the deal appeared to be hanging by a thread, McDonald jumped in. "I flew to Belgium on the spur of the moment for three days and hammered out some details. I got a better feel for them. I was on the ledge. But when I went over there, it changed things. It saved the deal. It gave me a chance to meet the Moortgat brothers, to meet some other people. We talked about employee benefits. You want your people taken care of."

More than the money, McDonald said he was concerned about the future of the brewery. "I was looking for an active partner that could bring a lot of things we didn't have, not really looking for a big brewery" to absorb Boulevard, he says.

"We're a little bit tired now. We just finished the transition. We have a much more interesting pool of people to pull ideas from. Going forward in the craft beer business is going to be tougher. Making good beer is just the table stakes," he says. "There is a lot of optimism. Amazing things are happening in the U.S. craft today; if you can figure it out, you can make a lot of money. Everyone wants local, but the business is more global than ever. Go figure."

The Foreseeable Future

The future for craft has never looked more promising, thanks in no small part to pioneers like Maytag and McDonald. Craft may have started out a ragtag sector, but many craft companies have grown into exemplary operations. The sector is maturing with example after example of smart, insightful operators growing their businesses in constructive, thoughtful ways. The more you learn about the craft beverage business—particularly craft beer—the more you find yourself wishing the rest of American business offered so much opportunity within such a collegial community.

Craft is, without a doubt, a more competitive environment than it was five years ago. But this sort of maturity sets an example for thriving in a wild and crazy business. The pieces are in place for a strong future for the sectors and for any craft business that launches now. It may never be a better time to start a craft company.

The wind will be at your back for the foreseeable future.

Craft Brewing, Distilling, and Cidering Resources

J ust as you can never have too many craft beverages from which to choose, you can also never have too many resources. Therefore, we present for your consideration a wealth of sources for you to check into, check out, and harness for your own personal information blitz as you prepare to make your mark in the craft industry. These resources will get you started on your research. They are by no means the only sources out there. We have done our research, but events, websites, and businesses—especially in the always growing and changing craft market—tend to move, change, fold, and expand. As we have repeatedly stressed, do your homework. Get out and start investigating.

Associations

American Craft Spirits Association
P.O. Box 217
Bloomington, IN 47402
(812) 325-6121
americancraftspirits.org

American Distilling Institute
P.O. Box 577
Hayward, CA 94541
(510) 886-7418
distilling.com

Brewers Association
1327 Spruce Street
Boulder, CO 80302
(303) 447-0816, toll free: (888) 822-6273
info@brewersassociation.org
brewersassociation.org

California Brewers Association
P.O. Box 807
Sacramento, CA 95812
(916) 228-4260
californiacraftbeer.com

Craft Brew Alliance
929 N. Russell Street
Portland, OR 97227
(503) 331-7270
contact@craftbrew.com
craftbrew.com

Florida Brewers Guild
P.O. Box 523
Cape Canaveral, FL 32920
(561) 463-2337
mike@duesouthbrewing.com
floridabrewersguild.org

Hop Growers of America
P.O. Box 1207
301 W. Prospect Place
Moxee, WA 98936
(509) 453-4749, fax: (509) 457-8561
info@usahops.org
usahops.org

Hop Research Council
P.O. Box 298
Hubbard, OR 97032
(503) 982-7600
info@hopresearchcouncil.org
hopresearchcouncil.org

National Beer Wholesalers Association
1101 King Street, Suite 600
Alexandria, VA 22314-2944
(703) 683-4300, toll free: (800) 300-6417, fax: (703) 683-8965
info@nbwa.org
www.nbwa.org

U.S. Association of Cider Makers
2650 W. 2nd Avenue, #10
Denver, CO 80219
ciderassociation.org

Market Trends and Craft Industry Websites

Artisan Spirit **Magazine**
P.O. Box 31494
Spokane, WA 99223
(509) 944-5919
brian@artisanspiritsmag.com
artisanspiritmag.com

Beer Marketer's Insights
49 E. Maple Avenue
Suffern, NY 10901

(845) 507-0040, fax: 845-507-0041

info@beerinsights.combeerinsights.com

BevNET.com Inc.

44 Pleasant Street, Suite 110

Watertown, MA 02472

(617) 231-8800

editorialnews@bevnet.com

bevnet.com

Brewbound

44 Pleasant Street, Suite 110

Watertown, MA 02472

(617) 231-8800

editorialnews@bevnet.com

brewbound.com

Brewpublic

P.O. Box 14525

Portland, OR 97293

(503) 449-4522

info@brewpublic

brewpublic.com

Craft Brewing Business

20691 Forestwood Drive

Strongsville, OH 44149

kgribbins@cbbmedia.com

craftbrewingbusiness.com

Hard Cider News

226 N. Fehr Way

Bay Shore, NY 11706

(631) 940-7290

info@starfishjunction.com

hardcidernews.com

Make Craft Cider

makecraftcider.com

Equipment Suppliers and Distributors

BrewCraft USA

3201 NW Lower River Road

Vancouver, WA 98660

21 Lawrence Paquette

Champlain, NY 12919

(360) 696-8356, (877) 355-2739

brewcraftusa.com

BSG CraftBrewing

800 West 1st Avenue

Shakopee, MN 55379

(800) 374-2739

Bsgcraftbrewing.com

DME Brewing Solutions

54 Hillstrom Avenue

Charlottetown, PE

Canada C1E 2C

(902) 628-6900

sales@dmebrewing.ca

dmebrewing.ca

Premier Stainless Systems

510 Corporate Drive, Unit D

Escondido, CA 92029

(760) 796-7999, fax: (760) 796-7905

info@premierstainless.com

premierstainless.com

ProBrewer.com

The eBay of brewing.

Real Beer Media Inc.

1459 18th Street, #287

San Francisco, CA 94107-2801

(650) 260-5178

www.probrewer.com

Southern Wine & Spirits of America
1600 NW 163rd Street
Miami, FL 33169
(305) 625-4171
southernwine.com

Wine Warehouse
6550 E. Washington Boulevard
Los Angeles, CA 90040
(800) 331-2829
winewarehouse.com

A Flight of Breweries, Distilleries, and Cider Makers

Alaskan Brewing Company
5429 Shaune Drive
Juneau, AK 99801-9540
(907) 780-5866, fax: (907) 780-4514
www.alaskanbeer.com

Albemarle CiderWorks
2545 Rural Ridge Lane
North Garden, VA 22959
(434) 297-2326
www.albemarleciderworks.com

Alchemy & Science
431 Pine Street, Suite G10
Burlington, VT 05401
alchemyandscience.com

Anchor Brewing Company
1705 Mariposa Street
San Francisco, CA 94107
(415) 863-8350, fax: (415) 552-7094
anchorbrewing.com

Balcones Distilling
212 S. 17th Street
Waco, TX 76701

(254) 755-6003

balconesdistilling.com

Bold Rock Hard Cider

1020 Rockfish Valley Highway (Rt. 151)

Nellysford, VA 22958

(434) 361-1030

boldrock.com

Boston Beer Company

One Design Center, Suite 850

Boston, MA 02210

(617) 368-5000

bostonbeer.com

Braxton Brewing Company

27 W. 7th

Covington, KY 41011

www.braxtonbrewing.com

Brooklyn Brewery

#1 Brewers Row, 79 N. 11th Street

Brooklyn, NY 11249

(718) 486-7422

brooklynbrewery.com

Brooks Dry Cider

3012 16th Street, Suite 210

San Francisco, CA 94103

(323) 369-0006

www.brooksdrycider.com

Cismontane Brewing Company

29851 Aventura

Rancho Santa Margarita, CA 92688

(949) 888-2739

cismontanebrewing.com

Denizens Brewing Company

1115 East-West Highway

Silver Spring, MD 20910

(301) 557-9818

denizenbrewingco.com

Dogfish Head Brewing Company

6 Cannery Village Center

Milton, DE 19968

(302) 226-BREW

dogfish.com

Dry Dock Brewing Company

15120 E. Hampden Avenue

Aurora, CO 80014

(303) 400-5606

drydockbrewing.com

Few Spirits

918 Chicago Avenue

Evanston, IL 60202

(847) 920-8628

info@fewspirits.com

fewspirits.com

Firestone Walker Brewing Company

1400 Ramada Drive

Paso Robles CA 93446

(805) 225-5911

firestonebeer.com

Founders Brewing Company

235 Grandville Avenue SW

Grand Rapids, MI 49503

(616) 776-2182

foundersbrewing.com

Four Saints Brewing Company

218 S. Fayetteville Street

Asheboro, NC 27203

(336) 560-7687

foursaintsbrewing.com

Gordon Biersch Brewing Company

357 E. Taylor Street

San Jose, CA 95112

(408) 278-1008, fax: (408) 278-1406

gordonbiersch.com

Grain Station Brew Works

755 NE Alpine Avenue

McMinnville, OR 97128

(503) 687-2739

www.grainstation.com

Grand Traverse Distillery

781 Industrial Circle, Suite 5

Traverse City, MI 49686

(231) 947-VODKA

info@grandtraversedistillery.com

grandtraversedistillery.com

Green Flash Brewing

6550 Mira Mesa Boulevard

San Diego, CA 92121

(858) 622-0085

info@greenflashbrew.com

www.greenflashbrew.com

Greenbar Craft Distillery

2459 E. 8th

Los Angeles, CA 90021

(213) 375-3668

greenbar.biz

Harlem Brewing Company

200 W. 138 Street

New York City, NY 10030

(888)559-6735

info@harlembrewing.com

harlembrewing.com

Jester King Brewery
13005 Fitzhugh Road, Building B
Austin, TX 78736
(512) 537-5100
info@jesterkingbrewery.com
jesterkingbrewery.com

June Lake Brewing Company
131 S. Crawford Avenue
June Lake, CA
(858) 668-6340
junelakebrewing.com

Kings County Distillery
Brooklyn Navy Yard, Building 121
63 Flushing Avenue, Box 379
Brooklyn, NY 11205
kingscountydistillery.com

Lagunitas
1280 N. McDowell Boulevard
Petaluma, CA 94954
(707) 769-4495
lagunitas.com

Mammoth Brewing Company
18 Lake Mary Road
Mammoth Lakes, CA 93546
(760) 934-7141
info@mammothbrewingco.com
www.mammothbrewingco.com

Modern Times Beer
3725 Greenwood Street
San Diego, CA 92110
(619) 546-9694
www.moderntimesbeer.com

New Belgium Brewing Company
500 Linden Street

Fort Collins, CO 80524
(970) 221-0524, toll free: (888) NBB-4044
www.newbelgium.com

New York Distilling Company
79 Richardson Street
Brooklyn, NY 11211
(718) 412-0874
info@nydistilling.com
nydistilling.com

Olde Saratoga Brewing Company
131 Excelsior Avenue
Saratoga Springs, NY 12866
(518) 581-0492
oldesaratogabrew.com

Russian River Brewing Company
725 4th Street
Santa Rosa, CA 95404
(707) 545-BEER
russianriverbrewing.com

Saint Arnold Brewing Company
2000 Lyons Avenue
Houston, TX 77020
(713) 686-9494, toll free: (800) 801-6402
saintarnold.com

St. George Spirits
2601 Monarch Street
Alameda, CA 94501
(510) 769-1601
stgeorgespirits.com

Sierra Nevada Brewing Company
1075 E. 20th Street
Chico, CA 95928
(530) 893-3520

info@sierranevada.com

sierranevada.com

Southern Tier Brewing Company

2072 Stoneman Circle

Lakewood, NY 14750

(716) 763-5479, fax: (716) 763-5489

stbcbeer.com

Stone Brewing Company

1999 Citracado Parkway

Escondido, CA 92029

(760) 294-7899

stonebrewing.com

Tandem Ciders

2055 N. Setterbo Road

Suttons Bay, MI 49682

(231) 271-0050

tandemciders.com

Tributary Brewing Company

10 Shapleigh Road

Kittery, ME 03904

(207) 703-0093

tributarybrewingcompany.com

Tuthilltown Spirits

14 Grist Mill Lane (P.O. Box 320)

Gardiner, NY 12525

(845) 255-1527

tuthilltown.com

Uinta Brewing

1722 Fremont Drive

Salt Lake City, UT 84104

(801) 467-0909

uintabrewing.com

Uncle John's Cider Mill & Fruit House Winery

8614 North US 127

St. John's, MI 48879
(989) 224-3686
hardcider.com

Virginia Beer Company
401 2nd Street
Williamsburg, VA 23185
www.virginiabeerco.com

Wildnerness Brewing Company
This brewery hasn't launched as yet. Their Kickstarter page is www.kickstarter.com/projects/1693254250/wilderness-brewing-co/description
www.wildernessbrewingco.com

Wormtown Brewery
455 Park Avenue
Worcester, MA 01610
(508) 239-1555
wormtownbrewery.com

Zero Gravity Craft Brewery
115 St. Paul Street
Burlington, VT 05401
(802) 861-2999
zerogravitybeer.com

National Craft Beer Festivals

American Craft Beer Week
When: Mid-May
Where: In brewpubs and small, independent craft breweries nationwide.
craftbeer.com/ACBW
Known as the Mother of all Beer Weeks, American Craft Beer Week celebrates craft brewers and craft beer culture in the U.S. It's a national celebration across the U.S. with events at breweries near you.

Great American Beer Festival
When: Late September
Where: Colorado Convention Center, Denver, CO

GreatAmericanBeerFestival.com

Three days long, with over 600 breweries and more than 3,000 beers to enjoy, this festival has been drawing tens of thousands of beer enthusiasts for over three decades. Purchase your tickets early, as the festival has sold out the past six years!

SAVOR: An American Craft Beer & Food Experience

When: Early June

Where: Washington, DC

savorcraftbeer.com

SAVOR is the main beer and food pairing event in the U.S. With 65 of the nation's top independent craft brewers participating, this is where beer enthusiasts and foodies can interact directly with some of the greatest brewers and brewery owners in the world.

National Homebrewers Conference and National Homebrew Competition

When: Mid-June

Where: San Diego, CA

AHAconference.org and HomebrewersAssociation.org

Join hundreds of homebrewers at the national conference for amateur brewers. Education and fun combine for a great experience!

Craft Spirit Festivals

Source: American Distilling Institute

American Distilling Institute (ADI) Spirits Conference & Vendor Expo

Anne Sophie Whitehead, Conference Director

P.O. Box 577

Hayward, CA 94541

(502) 299-0238

annesophie.whitehead@gmail.com

distilling.com

A gathering of craft distillers, industry experts, and suppliers, the conference includes four days of seminars, hands-on distilling workshops, tastings, and the annual awards ceremony for the "Judging of Artisan Spirits."

Art of the Cocktail

Victoria, British Columbia

11120 110 A Avenue

Edmonton, Alberta T5H 1K1

(250) 389-0444

sip@artofthecocktail.ca

artofthecocktail.ca

Art of the Cocktail is a three-day event showcasing all things cocktail. Supporting the craft cocktail movement and the educated consumer, it provides seminars, the Grand Tasting, and three competitions to immerse you in a spirited world.

Bite of Bend

Northwest Spirits & Mixology Show

P.O. Box 731

Bend, OR 97709

(503) 510-5603

Events@Drink-Think.net

nwspiritsshow.com

The NW Spirits and Mixology Show is the premier consumer event for craft distillers and mixologists. Held in Bend, Oregon, as a unique component of the Bite of Bend, the NWMS is an opportunity to build your brand with up to 25,000 consumers who come to the Northwest's pre-eminent playground.

Breckenridge Craft Spirits Festival

137 S. Main Street

Breckenridge, CO 80424

(907) 547-9759

breckenridgecraftspiritsfestival.com

A grand tasting of handcrafted spirits. Admission provides complimentary tasting glass, delicious craft spirits tasting, craft cocktails, people's choice voting, artisanal snacks, and live music.

Distill America

1001 Wisconsin Place

Madison, WI 91768

kevinguthrie80@gmail.com [Note: request pending for phone contact]

distillamerica.com

The folks organizing this event strive to open the public's heart and mind to the many facets of craft distillation. From the international giants to the boutique micro distillers, they want you to taste it all!

DSTILL
621 Kalamth Street
Denver, CO 80204
dstill-denver.com
This weeklong experience highlights American small-batch distilling with featured spirit tastings, craft cocktail events, and workshops highlighting top artisan distillers and bartenders from across the country.

Great American Distiller's Festival
101 N. Weidler Street
Portland, OR 97227
(503) 449-5680
distillersfestival.com
portlandcocktailweek.com
A gathering of small distillers from across the country who come to Oregon—the Mecca of craft distilling, to share their products, passion, and expertise in handcrafting spirits. The event is in conjunction with Portland Cocktail Week and includes tastings, seminars, mixology contests for bartenders, and much, much more!

Independent Spirits Expo
Chicago, IL
P.O. Box 781
Westport, CT 06881
(203) 226-4181
indiespirits@gmail.com
indiespiritsexpo.com
The largest gathering of small, independent, family-owned, handcrafted spirits and the distillers, importers, bottlers, distributors, and representative under one roof! Sample some of the best of the boutique vodkas, gins, rums, tequilas, mescals, whiskies, and liqueurs from all around the world.

Kentucky Bourbon Festival
One Court Square
Bardstown, KY 40004
Linda Harrison, Executive Director
(502) 348-3623, toll free: (800) 638-4877 #4, fax: (502) 348-3403
kybourbonfestival.com

info@kybourbonfestival.com

Celebrating one of the world's finest spirits in the bourbon capital of the world.

London Cocktail Week

info@londoncocktailweek.com

londoncocktailweek.com

A unique celebration of our capital's unrivalled cocktail culture—through a host of seminars, pop-up bars, tastings parties, and master classes held throughout the city. Aimed at both novices and experienced professionals. London Cocktail Week will inspire, educate, and unite cocktail lovers.

Los Angeles International Spirits Expo

Los Angeles Convention Center

1201 S. Figueroa Street

Los Angeles, CA 90015

laspiritsexpo.com

Los Angeles International Spirits Expo is an ideal destination that helps the professionals and experts of the sector to connect and interact with each other and also enhances the ideal opportunities and new developments that help the growth and expansion of the industry.

Manhattan Cocktail Classic

344 Atlantic Avenue, #A1

Brooklyn, NY 11201

info@manhattancocktailclassic.com

manhattancocktailclassic.com

Part festival, part fête, part conference, part cocktail party—the Manhattan Cocktail Classic is an annual celebration of the myriad points of intersection between cocktails and culture. With nearly 100 events spread across five days and four boroughs—and a multi-day trade conference to boot—the Manhattan Cocktail Classic offers a vast array of unique experiences to enthusiasts and professionals alike, expanding the very definition of what constitutes a "cocktail event."

Nashville Whiskey Festival

2225th Avenue S.

Nashville, TN 37203

nashvillewhiskeyfestival.com

The Nashville Whiskey Festival culminates with the Grand Tasting at the Country Music Hall of Fame and Museum. This event features approximately 70 distillers pouring product and offering educational seminars. There will also be a cigar bar, an outdoor pavilion, and a full spread of snacks available throughout the evening.

Philadelphia Whiskey & Fine Spirits

1818 Market Street

Philadelphia, PA 19103

phillymag.com/whiskeyfest

The Grand Tasting will feature over 200 premium spirits from around the world, including whiskey, scotch, bourbon, tequila, gin, rum, and vodka. Guests can converse with industry representatives, try cuisine from Philadelphia's best restaurants, and enjoy lounges and entertainment.

Pittsburgh Whiskey & Fine Spirits Festival

777 Casino Drive

Pittsburgh, PA 15212

(412) 281-2681

pittsburghwhiskeyfestival.com

The Pittsburgh Whiskey & Fine Spirits Festival is nationally recognized as one of the top five whiskey events in the country. On hand will be more than 300 varieties of whiskey, scotch, vodka, gin, rum, tequila, and cordials, all laid out by the finest purveyors of distilled spirits from around the world. They'll be served up by some of the most knowledgeable distillers and mixologists in the industry.

Portland Cocktail Week

1001 SE Water Street, Suite 225

Portland, OR 97214

info@pdxcw.com

(513) 760-5874

portlandcocktailweek.com

Portland Cocktail Week brings skilled bartenders, spirits professionals, and cocktail enthusiasts to the heart of Stumptown for education and camaraderie!

San Diego Spirits Festival

1000 N. Harbor Drive

San Diego, CA 92101

(858) 551-1605

info@SanDiegoSpiritsFestival.com

sandiegospiritsfestival.com

San Diego Spirits Festival is the major cocktail, culinary, and cultural extravaganza celebrated annually each summer on San Diego Bay. The goal is to advance the industry and all that it encompasses via market launches, industry advancement and exposure, product innovation, education, and of course, a good time filled with entertainment, camaraderie, and just good fun.

Tales of the Cocktail
538 Louisa Street
New Orleans, LA 70117
Ann Tunnerman, Founder
Christina Gaspari, Event Manager
(504) 948-0511
Ann@talesofthecocktail.com
Christina@talesofthecocktail.com
TalesoftheCocktail.com
Join Tunnerman and Gaspari in New Orleans for five days—where the cocktail reigns supreme. All hail the cocktail!

Whiskies of the World
San Francisco, San Jose, Houston, Atlanta, and Austin
168 Park Bolton Place
San Jose, CA 95136
(408) 225-0446
Lana Chizhik-Smith
cs@whiskiesoftheworld.com
whiskiesoftheworld.com
Whiskies of the World organizes whiskey tasting events with brands across the globe attending and showcasing their latest releases. We welcome consumers and the trade alike to our events and we promote whiskey knowledge and appreciation. Whiskies of the World is part of the IWSC Group.

WHISKYFest
Chicago, New York, San Francisco
Whisky Advocate Magazine
P.O. Box 37850
Boone, IA 50037
(610) 967-1083

whiskyadvocate.com/whiskyfest

Offers whiskey enthusiasts the opportunity to sample from more than 200 rare and exclusive whiskies from around the world, savor gourmet food, and attend seminars by distillery managers and master blenders.

WHISKYLIVE

King Street House

15 Upper King Street

Norwich, England

NR3 1RB

44 (0) 1603 633808

whiskylive.com

An international celebration of whiskey with a unique opportunity to sample the greatest whiskies in the world while mingling with the producers, distillers, and marketers. Sample rare and sought-after whiskies and meet the stars of the industry.

Craft Beverage Expo

When: May

Where: California

Executive Director: Kellie Shevlin

Kellie@craftbeverageexpo.com

Craftbeverageexpo.com

As the number-one event dedicated to the business of craft beverage, Craft Beverage Expo unites all craft producers, including artisan wine, craft beer, cider, spirits, and mead. The three-day event celebrates collaboration, highlights innovation, and showcases the best and next practices across all segments of this vibrant community.

Glossary

Big Beer: blanket term for large beer companies. AB-InBev and SABMiller are the parent companies of America's largest beer producers, Anheuser-Busch and MillerCoors, respectively. When this book refers to "Big Beer," it is a reference to these two companies.

Big Spirits: blanket term for large spirit companies. Diageo overwhelmingly dominates the American spirits industry. But Pernod Ricard, Bacardi, Beam Suntory, Brown-Forman, and Gruppo Campari are also major spirits producers. When this book refers to "Big Spirits," it refers to all these companies.

Craft Alcoholic Beverage Industry: general term used to describe independently owned breweries, distilleries, and cideries that create alcoholic beverages using small batch methods. In this book, we are concerned with American beer, spirits, and hard cider. The "craft alcoholic beverage industry" is a term we use as a matter of convenience. You won't find it used this way elsewhere.

For one thing, "craft" doesn't have a specific definition. "Craft" typically refers to producers who aren't "big;" however it doesn't mean these are "small" producers. The various "craft" trade associations define "craft" differently. Regional producers, such as Yuengling Brewery, increasingly are included under the "craft" umbrella even though they have been around for centuries and make more product than any of the younger companies typically identified as "craft." Technically, wine should be included as a craft alcoholic beverage; however, it is beyond the scope of this book.

Craft Brewery: independently owned (less than 25 percent of the craft brewery is owned or controlled by an alcoholic beverage industry member that is not itself a craft brewer), producing no more than 6 million barrels of beer a year. Embracing European traditions, craft brewers use malted grains and fresh hops to revive old styles as well as to invent new ones.

Craft Cidery: independently owned cider production facility. Because the American hard cider industry is just starting to gain traction, there are tiny, small, smaller, and very fast growing cideries. The meaningful difference between cideries is not their size; rather it is the ingredients in the cider they produce. If hard cider includes apple juice concentrate or added sugars or preservatives, it is referred to as "industrial" hard cider in this book.

For the purposes of this book, "artisan" hard cider is fresh fruit juice—typically apples, quince and pears—and is often an orchard-centered operation.

Craft Distillery: as defined by The American Craft Spirits Association, craft distillers are independent, licensed distillers annually producing fewer than 750,000 proof gallons of spirits.

Three-Tier System: The repeal of Prohibition introduced new rules for the distribution and sale of alcoholic beverages, requiring producers to operate separately from distributors, which operated separately from retailers, thus the three-tier system. Each state established its own set of rules for the three-tier system. With the craft movement, most states have waived some of these rules for small producers. But for the vast majority of producers, the three-tier system still governs the overall sale and distribution of alcoholic beverages.

Index